Our Dangerous Friend

Bushfire Philosophy
in
South West Australia

David Jefford Ward

Published by
The Book Reality Experience
Western Australia
*

Table of Contents

Dedication

Although some essays have only indirect relevance to them, this book is dedicated to the *Noongar* people of south-west Australia, because I regard them as the rightful traditional custodians of the south-west forests, heaths, and wetlands, and they should be a respected source of information for our present and future bushfire philosophy, ecology, and management.

I have met occasional grumpiness in my attempts to contact them, but I know enough about *Noongar* history to understand why, and offer my support. I have walked in the bush with Elders in the past, and would gladly accept any further invitation from them to *danjoo koorliny* (walk together) about *karla* (fire). I hope some of the more thoughtful politicians, managers, and scientists will walk with us too, if they haven't already. Perhaps some are afraid of burning their toes.

We all have a responsibility to make bushfire our friend again, rather than the fashionable news media monster of a devilish enemy, who can supposedly be triumphantly defeated, if only our governments would buy enough trucks, aircraft, computer software, pink fire retardant, and other costly, and photogenic technology.

As an insight into that view of bushfire, at an international fire conference in Sydney, I found myself on a table with a salesman for such equipment. He had clear opinions on Australian bushfire, with no doubt that it should be managed in a military style, as in the USA. Technology, and perhaps profits, seemed to rule his brain.

On the other hand, a literate American anthropologist, Professor Rebecca Bliege Bird, who has studied traditional use of fire with Aboriginal people in the Northern Territory for some years, has a different fire philosophy. She has put it succinctly as '*Tradition Trumps Technology*'.

If I refer to *karl ngara* (traditional burning) in these essays, I hope I have got it right. Although over eighty years old, I am only a beginner.

-oOo-

Preface

Good foresight needs good insight into hindsight.

Apocryphal Irish Proverb

That Irish philosopher, Spike Milligan, once claimed that Irish people think sideways, and he was a fluent exponent of it. Whether sideways, backward or forward, I think the above alleged proverb is true, but may not be understood by those who glibly dismiss bushfire history and philosophy; or are bedazzled by the rhetoric and glamour of scientific *'refereed papers'*, and *'models'*; or are otherwise a bit slow on the uptake. This collection of essays is often based on historical hindsights, which may give insight into a clear, cheerful, and all round better foresight into Australian bushfire.

Over fifty years ago I was employed by the former West Australian Forests Department as a workman (Grade 4), and was given a humble role, under qualified foresters, in lighting, suppressing, and doing research into, bushfires in the *karri* forest and pine plantations of south-west Australia. I measured wind speeds, fuel quantity and moisture content, then statistically related them to flame height and rate of spread. None of this work was published in refereed papers, partly because I was, at that time, not literate enough to write them. Another reason was that a then Conservator of Forests considered that those who had time to publish papers obviously did not have enough real work to do. Having read some recent *'peer reviewed papers'* on bushfire, I think he had a point.

More recently, as a research scientist in the 1990s, I found black fire marks under the charcoal on the stems of many old *balga* grasstrees, giving some hindsight into fire frequency back to the 1700s, before European settlers arrived. Chemical analysis and histology of these black marks has confirmed that they are the records of past fires.

There have been attempts at discrediting the *balga* work, by using satellite data, statistics and computer models, all regarded by some as unquestionable evidence. Yet the fire intervals on old *balga* trees match

iii

perfectly well with evidence from old letters, journals, newspaper articles, and conversations with *Noongar* Elders. Satellite data, statistics, and computer models can be right, but should always be questioned. Under careful and persistent questioning, the truth will emerge.

In the essays I mention few names of *Noongar* Elders, because some of them have since passed on, I hope happily to *Kooranup* (heaven?), over the Indian Ocean. Some I contacted through the former Department of Conservation and Land Management, and others through meetings kindly arranged by Julie Jones, of the former West Australian Department of Aboriginal Affairs.

I thank those *Noongar* people who have given me information. Even if not named, those still alive know who they are. I understand their reticence in revealing traditional knowledge to publication hungry *wadjela* (whitefella) academics. As a *wadjela* myself, I have long enjoyed the old *Noongar* stories of Dr Noel Nannup.

David Ward
Bridgetown
December 2021

Essay 1

Verily, Lord Verulam…

> *'I have taken all knowledge to be my province.'*
> Francis Bacon, Lord Verulam, Viscount St Albans,
> *Eloquent Philosopher and Scientist, 1561-1626*

As we may see above, Francis Bacon had but modest aims and interests. He was one of the first to promote the scientific method, yet he also loved the bible. According to some he contributed to the eloquence of the King James version of the bible, published in 1611. Some experts deny this, and they may be right, but I am sure he clearly recognized its emphasis on wisdom, a handmaiden of real science.

In Ecclesiastes, we meet the eloquent simile, possibly penned by Francis, that *'Wisdom exceedeth folly, as far as light excelleth darkness.'* In understanding important matters such as bushfire management and ecology, we should surely seek intellectual light, to avoid misleading darkness. Yet, in today's academic career chase, readers can be confused by competing academic ambitions, sometimes promoted by rhetoric, or muddled by misleading reasoning. Sadly, some people say that an academic expert is someone who has held up research by others for at least fifteen years. I hope I am not one of those experts, but if I can shed historical and philosophical light on some bushfire folly, I shall be happy.

In 1625 Francis Bacon published a book of essays, long applauded for shedding philosophical light upon a wide range of human affairs. He was not the first, or only essayist to do so in western culture, some others being such French scholars as Michel de Montaigne, and classical writers like Plutarch and Cicero. For example, Cicero believed that *'To be ignorant of what occurred before you were born is to remain always a child'*. This surely applies to those who publish papers on bushfire, with no reference to its history.

Bacon's essays are short and pithy. Regrettably, it seems the pithiness

1

came at a cost. According to a recent eminent commentator, the late Lord Anthony Quinton, Bacon's wife Alice complained about his *'enigmatical, folded writing'*. Present day readers of Bacon's essays may still have occasional difficulty with this enigmatic approach, but it sometimes takes repeated reading to unfold it, and the effort is worthwhile.

Although I surely lack Francis Bacon's eloquence, I have adopted his essay approach in this book, in the belief that the logic of a cross disciplinary approach to bushfire understanding is more valid than the narrow claim that only *'refereed papers in scientific journals'* should be believed. I suspect that some such papers about bushfire, by botanists and zoologists, are, on their own, incompetent to understand the complexities of that cross disciplinary matter. I hope that essays might, even if by shock tactics, be a way of achieving more cautious respect and cooperation between what are sometimes seen today as separate and competing forms of knowledge. This sad rupture between science and humanities was spotted in the nineteen fifties by a scientist, Charles Percy Snow, in his book about *'Two Cultures'*, and the dispute continues. Claims of superiority by one *'culture'* or another need to be abolished, and the need for both to be recognised. This also applies, in Australia, to the three lane highway of natural science, humanities, and Aboriginal memory. Philosophy might help us along that road too.

Some Australian politicians, perhaps admiring a certain type of scientist, or a certain type of education, have urged the adoption of an education based on STEM (science, technology, engineering, mathematics), but others, I suspect better educated, urge the inclusion of the arts and humanities, preferring the acronym STEAM. These better educated people must be well aware, for example, of the connection between music, and mathematics, and the vital role of clear language in logical thinking, and in the clear expression of scientific findings.

Bereft of arts and humanities, mediated by philosophy, we may increasingly face a barren desert of poorly worded science, with difficulty in distinguishing dark folly from the light of truth. I think this may already apply to some bushfire theories allegedly based solely on natural science, as if such a thing were possible.

Probably due to long and deep thinking, Francis Bacon's writing has a rather grave nature, so, by contrast, I make a few attempts at humour in my own essays, yet trying to avoid folly. I also try to avoid enigmatic, or *'folded'* writing.

Perhaps some present day folded writing in natural science is fostered by misplaced conceit, due to the greater use of mathematical analysis, especially inductive statistics, in that area, but we should not forget that

2

mathematics is not itself a science. It is certainly a useful tool of science, but is itself a branch of logic, which is a major branch of philosophy, a branch of thinking which is oddly despised by some less thoughtful natural scientists.

Disappointingly, the natural science literature on bushfire has become fractious, due to differing ideologies on nature becoming publicly confused with science, sometimes by the use of rhetoric, posing as logic. Aristotle noticed this misleading use of false logic long ago. Yet some present natural scientists seem to be unaware of his views.

I believe successful bushfire management needs to be philosophically based on a rich experience of practical application, and humanities such as history, supported both by social and natural sciences. I hope the cross disciplinary essay will, increasingly, be used as a tool to create such a rich understanding. If unchallenged, present trends in some claimed bushfire science are unlikely to bring us to a sound understanding, and hence competent bushfire management. Without such an understanding, the management of landscape fire will prove increasingly difficult, costly, and dangerous. Politicians should ponder the potential effect upon their reputations of believing bad bushfire science, even if written by academics with impressive strings of academic qualifications, and shoals of refereed publications.

In stimulating contrast to the problematic *'refereed scientific literature'* approach to bushfire is the concept of *'songlines'*, a form of musical, artistic, even poetic oral encyclopaedia, long used by Australian Aboriginal people as a memory code to describe their country, and teach its history, ownership, ecology, food and water sources, and fire management, to young people. I have read that some present day Aboriginal paintings use songline themes. The use of art, songs, colour and dance definitely falls into the mind set of STEAM, not STEM.

In western literature the topic of songlines was raised, in the 1980s, by the English writer Bruce Chatwin, and more recently by the Australian Aboriginal writer Margo Neale. I am aware of a third writer, Lynne Kelly, author of *'The Memory Code'*, a book suggesting that the method used by Australian Aboriginal people was also widely used in other parts of the world and cultures, for example near the site of neolithic Stonehenge, on Salisbury Plain, in England, and in American Indian culture.

I do not deeply explore songlines in this book, because I do not know enough about them. It would be most useful for other writers, Aboriginal or not, to investigate the potential role of songlines in bushfire ecology and management. Quite recently (2021), Margo Neale and Lynne Kelly have *'walked together'* in an absorbing book on the subject, which I recommend as a background to anybody interested in deep knowledge systems, including bushfire management. It may be necessary to fight off the thinking of those academics who still believe in a shallow form of published natural science as the only trustworthy source of information in such matters, often ignoring Aboriginal fire knowledge, or cherry picking it for rhetorical purposes.

My former, and much respected colleague Dr. Noel Nannup OAM, once produced a map of what he called 'Dreaming Trails' in south-west Australia. Knowing the rate of litter deposition and plant growth there as I do, regular, deliberate burning must have been a part of this dreaming, if only to enable walking along such trails. The trails, and burning, had, of course, many other purposes. If we knew the songs and stories associated with the dreaming trails, or songlines, of the south-west corner of Australia, we might learn much about bushfire, plants, and animals too, but of course this would be intruding into, and possibly exploiting, *Noongar* culture. Some Elders may, understandably, prefer to keep this information to themselves, given that it has been so long ignored by many scientists of European ancestry. As a simple example, why call a plant *Xanthorrhoea preissii* (yellow flowing of Mr. Preiss?) when it was surely not discovered by Mr. Preiss, but has been known for millennia, by the *Noongar* name *balga*?

If we use his cross disciplinary essay approach, might Lord Verulam help to bridge the gap between western and Aboriginal culture, at least on bushfire? That is to say the gap between sometimes shallow, one-eyed statistical models, and enchanting, colourful songlines, developed over tens of thousands of years by practical experience, out of love and respect for the land?

At my age, I gladly look forward to others tackling this approach, but I will help if I can. I understand that '*bidi-bidi*' is the *Noongar* language for footpaths, and also the term for the veins and arteries of our bodies. An intriguing thought, which I discuss further in Essay 18, in collaboration with the eighteenth century Italian philosopher, Giovanni Battista Vico.

-oOo-

Essay 2

Is Bushfire our Friend or Foe?

'A man cannot be too careful in the choice of his enemies.'
Oscar Wilde, *The Picture of Dorian Grey (1891)*

Some people blame the current troublesome nature of bushfires in Australia entirely on global warming, predicted by mathematical models. Those of a *'logical positivist'* tendency may support that view ferociously, scorning all others. For them, natural science and computer models are the only parents of truth. But is present climate science the truth, the whole truth, and nothing but the truth? It has been contradictory before, for example in the nineteen-seventies. If I remember correctly the news media then reported the prediction, by science, of a dangerously cooling climate due to industrial pollution and atomic explosions. As mentioned in Essay 1, the Roman Marcus Tullius Cicero had an opinion on those who are ignorant of the past.

The climate of south-west Australia has certainly been, on average, unusually dry for the past few decades, although the recent winter (2021) was, where I live, wetter and colder than any I can remember. There has been snow on the *Porongorup* hills six times in the current year, which is very unusual. Yet something else has changed too. Over the past fifty years at least, the quantity and connectivity of dead fuel in the bush has visibly increased due to a blatant decline in deliberate, skilled burning by humans. In particular, the former ancient art of burning by the *Noongar* folk of south-west Australia has been almost ignored by most of our politicians, scientists, and public servants for nearly two centuries.

Some early European settlers in the Swan River Colony, in the 1830s, did not understand, and were much irritated by, the traditional and frequent summer bushfires lit by *Noongar* people. The settlers were greatly annoyed at the loss of grazing for their imported sheep and cattle. In 1846 they persuaded the Governor to pass a law forbidding traditional frequent

5

burning by *Noongar* people on pain of flogging, and imprisonment on Rottnest Island, sometimes in itself a death sentence (see Essay 6).

Soon after the arrival of European settlers, some *Noongars* died of imported scarlet fever and influenza. Later, particularly in 1860 and the early 1880s, the burning ban was augmented by a sharp decline in *Noongar* numbers, due to deaths from measles, to which *Noongars* had little immunity (Essay 7). These diseases came from England, like me, other settlers, sheep, cattle, and later rabbits.

More recently there has been opposition to deliberate burning from some voluble and much published academic scientists, contradicting, ignoring, or cherry picking the views of *Noongar* people, those of some early European settlers, and some of our earlier scientists, whose ideas were based on extensive field observations, on foot or horseback. Yet close and careful observation, reliable assumptions, and careful logic, including when appropriate, statistics, are the very basis of good science.

Although it is now near compulsory to use statistics in a scientific paper, it has not always been so. In his great work on evolution, Charles Darwin used, as far as I can remember, no statistical analysis, which was only developed later by such pioneers as Adolphe Quetelet, Francis Galton, Karl Pearson, and Sir Ronald Fisher. Nor did Darwin drive a utility truck on his field trips. He was a great walker, and the view on foot, or from horseback, is much richer, and more intimate, than the view through a car windscreen. *Noongar* people were, of course, also great walkers on their *bidi-bidi*, or Dreaming Trails, and must have observed a great deal over many thousands of years.

A colleague, Dr Lachie McCaw, has pointed out that one of the earliest European bushfire scientists, the West Australian Colonial Botanist, James Drummond (1787-1863), once sent a letter to the Director of Kew Gardens, in London, who was having difficulty growing West Australian plants. Drummond advised him to prune the plants, and give them some ashes, as a substitute for the three to four year burning they received in their native land. He said that many West Australian plants only flowered well the year after they were burnt, and that is still true. He could have mentioned the benefits of fire to some edible *fungi* too.

In 1957, Charles A. Gardner, who had been Government Botanist since 1929, wrote an article for the Western Australian Naturalist. He described the common occurrence of fire in West Australian vegetation, and gave his opinion that *'absolute protection from fire in the thicket formations has a detrimental effect on the vegetation.'*

The decrease in burning frequency over the twentieth century was due to a number of reasons, one being some misleading ideas, starting with the first West Australian Conservator of Forests, Charles Lane-Poole, on his appointment in 1916. He followed the muddled advice on fire given by his forestry mentor, Sir David Hutchins (Essay 4), who had recommended Lane-Poole's appointment.

During Lane-Poole's brief tenure, he tried to banish all forest burning, but predictably failed due to lightning and locomotives. His successor, Stephen Kessel, tried minimal burning of five chain breaks around the edge of forest blocks, hoping to leave the interiors unburnt. According to some Annual Reports of the then Forests Department, in the 1920s, this often involved the deliberate destruction by axe of many old *balga* grasstrees in those breaks. No account was taken of the fact that *balga* were, and still are, of great importance to *Noongar* people. Yet, partly due to the highly flammable thatch of the remaining *balga*, fires still regularly escaped into the long unburnt interiors of forest blocks.

This hopeless defensive fire break attitude was reversed by a later Conservator of Forests, Alan C. Harris, after four forest workers were killed by fire near Nannup in 1958, and the particularly fierce fires in long unburnt forests at Dwellingup and other places a few years later, in the hot summer of 1961. Knowing of the previous failure of five chain breaks, he tried burning large areas of the *jarrah* forest at 3-4 year intervals. It was still well-known at that time that *Noongar* people had done so prior to World War 1. Even David Hutchins, an opponent of forest burning, recognised that the *jarrah* forest had long been burnt at intervals of 3-4 years, and said so in 1916, although he believed his version of '*science*' was superior to that of '*natives*' (Essay 4).

A later Conservator of Forests, Roy Wallace, was once president of the Royal Society of WA. In an article in their journal (1966) he wrote that '...*it is not unreasonable to assume that the forest was completely burnt through every 2-4 years. Even as late as 1925 the writer was able to observe three fires of this nature in unmanaged virgin forest east of Jarrahdale. These fires were alight in December and continued to burn until the following March.*' Recent *balga* grasstree cleaning (2003) in Monadnocks Conservation Park, east of Jarrahdale, has shown old fire marks at 2-4 year intervals there from 1750 up to the 1920s. Some of these were in *wandoo* forest, which will carry a fire every two years.

The Forests Department burnt on the basis of forest blocks, based on logging coups. Burning at 2-4, or 3-4 years made the work in heavy fuel too difficult, so the fire interval was simplistically doubled to 6-8 years, and remained so for decades. Yet, due to the heavy fuels, these longer intervals were only effective in some places and some kind of weather, and there were escapes.

Great credit is due to the Bushfire Front of Western Australia, an organisation of retired foresters with combined centuries of real fire experience between them. Based on this real fire experience, for decades they have demanded more well managed precautionary burning, and, following a number of severe bushfires in south-west Australia, and a lot of stamina on their part, seem at last to be getting some traction in the West Australian political arena. I say '*seem*' because political opinions can change according to political breezes, bearing news media campaigns.

One factor in this current traction may be the finding by some economists that it is actually cheaper to carry out frequent, deliberate, pre-emptive burning, than to fight enormous wildfires with helicopters and jumbo jets. It is also certainly safer and more ecologically helpful, if we want to restore and maintain large parts of *Noongar boodja* (country) in something like its condition before European settlement first took place.

Credit must also go to those present young officers of the strangely named West Australian Department of Biodiversity, Conservation, and Attractions (DBCA) who have taken up the challenge of fire management, in cooperation with the Department of Fire and Emergency Services (DFES). They have done some useful research, and gained useful experience, but might pay more attention to the humanistic and historical aspects of *Noongar* fire knowledge.

An important role should also be played by local government fire officers, but they are sometimes handicapped, or hoodwinked, by the misguided views of some councillors, or some members of the public. Seemingly educated by television, or eco-gossip, these opponents of regular burning believe that fire is always an enemy, to be suppressed when it occurs, and never deliberately lit to reduce fuel loads and rejuvenate the vegetation. They sometimes imbibe these views from those academics who seem to base their beliefs on a combination of ideology, statistics and computer models, rather than actual fire experience and grasp of fire history.

When I look out of my window at Bridgetown, I sometimes see smoke coming over the hill between here and Manjimup, due to the efforts by DBCA and DFES crews to protect both society and nature from holocaust fires in the coming summer. Such burning needs courage, cool heads, careful planning, and a practical understanding of the matter, far surpassing the theories of some much published '*bushfire experts*'.

The Greek philosopher, Plato, once distinguished between popular conjecture (*doxa*), written knowledge (*episteme*) and practical knowledge (*gnosis*). As an example, no student pilot should trust a flying instructor who has read, and thought, a great deal about flying; has attended and given lectures on it; sat for hours in those models known as flight simulators; and even had photographs taken in a flying suit, but has never actually been off the ground. Further, I believe the Arabs, who gleaned much philosophy from the Greeks, have a saying that *The tongue of experience has the most truth.'*

The present existence of large areas of dangerous, long unburnt forest and heath is also the result of some other human aspects, including the loss, due to age, poorly conceived Public Service redundancy schemes, or professional disgust, of experienced bushfire practitioners from government departments, especially at the time of the politically motivated abolition of the former Department of Conservation and Land Management (CALM). After a bewildering number of name changes in the past few decades (Forests Department, CALM, DOC, DEC, DPAW), this is currently known as the Department of Biodiversity, Conservation and Attractions (DBCA). I assume each change had a deep political, scientific, or even philosophical significance which eludes me, and probably cost a lot of public money in repainting vehicles, printing new stationery etc. I suspect that any long serving public servants still in those departments must be a little shell shocked.

Amidst the rhetorical, political, ideological, administrative, and academic jumble, the fact remains that fire has long been the friend of humans, keeping us warm in long past ice ages, and helping with hunting and cooking. Our transport system still depends on the internal combustion engine, albeit with the penalty of air pollution and heating. I hope electric cars can help us in that matter, although I believe their range is not yet sufficient for some Australian journeys. Some cultures identify fire as an essential element of the earth's ecosystem. As I understand it, *Noongar* people still see fire as a powerful and important friend, who can be dangerous if neglected. It would be good to hear directly, and publicly, from them on this fundamental philosophical outlook on bushfire management.

There is a great need for more research into the benefits of frequent, mild, patchy bushfire, and an equally great need for the effective communication of the findings to the public, especially school children, who may be sometimes misled by sensational news media reports, or the more ideological members of the teaching profession.

The friendly benefits of frequent, mild, patchy fire include reduction of fuel quantity and connectivity, and hence of potential fire intensity and spread; greater safety for humans and their property; creation of a diverse mosaic of habitat for native plants, and the wild animals which feed upon, and live amongst them; release of nutrients which otherwise remain locked up in dead organic matter; stimulation of flowering and seed germination; reduction of dense toxic smoke episodes; and the creation and reactivation of beneficial charcoal in the soil. Bushfire reduces the acidity of some soils, at least for a few years, so immobilising potential toxins such as aluminium and copper. Less acid conditions, due to combined white ash (*yoort*) and soil charcoal (*kop*) promote some beneficial soil bacteria and cyanobacteria.

I hope that some *Noongar* Elders are trying to promote such benefits, under the wider title of *danjoo koorliny*, or *'walking together'*. If they are, I wish them every good fortune. They will succeed eventually, but it remains a matter of time for the penny to drop, in some parts of Australian society, that fire is a friend, even if a dangerous one. Before the penny does drop, we may have to suffer further vast and dangerous bushfires.

I have mentioned that I have great respect for the skills of old foresters, and both professional and volunteer fire fighters. Yet when it comes to a holistic understanding of fire ecology, my money is on the Aboriginal Elders and their deeper traditional knowledge. I am happy to read well written papers on the subject, but don't need to read any more poorly written, yet refereed ones, which do not convince me as true. Yet I can see the truth shining out of the Elders' faces.

-oOo-

Essay 3

Bushfire, Ecology, Truth, & Lamp Posts

> *'As often as a study is cultivated by narrow minds,*
> *they will draw from it narrow conclusions.'*
>
> John Stuart Mill, Philosopher 1806-1873

Promotion in academia seems sometimes to be based on the number of publications, or even the number of pages published. I once briefly worked for a university, where a professor encouraged me to engage in *'salami publishing'*, that is to say dividing each piece of research into as many publications as possible. I did not follow his advice, and perhaps as a result, did not stay there long. Luckily, I met other, wiser professors who helped me, in my seventies, to complete a thesis on bushfire.

Another academic tactic for fame and promotion is to assemble a large team of co-authors. This is greatly helped by the advent of email. I have seen a paper with forty such co-authors, geographically scattered. I cannot believe that they all made significant contributions, but they doubtless claimed the paper in their academic publication count.

Another advantage of including so many sleeping partners is that the names of some may already be widely published and known in the field, and so improve the probability of acceptance by certain journal referees, who may happen to know them. Yet it has been said, by some more discerning scholars, that those who publish the most, sometimes have the least to say.

Nevertheless, I admire genuine scholars. The three I am thinking of at present were, perhaps significantly, all educated at Oxford University. They are the late Mary Midgley, a philosopher: Peter Checkland, a professor interested in complex, multidisciplinary problems, involving humans, and their differing views of the world: and the earliest of them, a wise old man called Sir Geoffrey Vickers VC, who fought in two world wars, and is credited with initiating Operations Research. This is rated by some as one

11

of the three major innovations to come out of the Second World War. The other two were radar and the nuclear bomb. Sadly, not all innovations are good and useful, but some are.

I doubt if Mary ever saw an Australian bushfire, yet she is remembered as a clear thinker, and some of her ideas might help sort out the muddled thinking about bushfire research, management and ecology. My immediate debt to Margaret is her reminder, in one of her books, of the old joke about a drunk, at night, searching diligently for his car keys under a lamp post. A passer by asks him if that is where he dropped them, and he says '*No, but it's the easiest place to look*'. This metaphor can be elaborated by imagining that several other people, drunk or sober, may also have dropped keys in that area, some near the lamp, and some in the dark. The drunk, or people trying to help him, may find some keys, but they may, or may not, be the keys they are looking for.

Perish the thought that I see all natural scientists, who work on bushfire, as fumbling drunks unable to find any keys, or finding the wrong ones. There has been some excellent work. Some do, however, have a tendency to confine themselves to searching under the lamp of what they call *hard science*, usually their particular branch of natural science, such as botany or zoology, much embellished with statistical paraphernalia. They can be hostile, and even sneer at those of us who undertake a wider search for bushfire truth, perhaps in the social sciences, or in the even wider, and sometimes intellectually demanding areas of history, philosophy, anthropology, and archaeology. One of the richest search areas, yet little explored, is in the memories of current Aboriginal Elders and early settler families. I have already (Essay 1) mentioned the potential importance of song lines.

Not all natural scientists are entirely hostile to those intellectually demanding areas. For example, a well-known American entomologist, Edward O. Wilson, once described the social sciences as '*hypercomplex*', and '*inherently far more difficult than physics and chemistry*'. For this reason he suggested that social sciences, not physics and chemistry, should be called the '*hard sciences*'.

I note, however, that Edward also confusingly suggested that the methods of natural science should replace those of the '*crumbling*' humanities, in other words we should search only under the various lamp posts of natural science. I don't think that is good advice. By doing so, we might overlook some important keys. The enlightened areas of natural science are wonderfully big, but the occasionally shadowy areas of the humanities may be even bigger. Physics is a wonderful science, but physics envy, and thoughtless imitation of its methods, can be an intellectual dead

12

end for other kinds of thinkers.

Returning to Professor Peter Checkland, I believe that his thinking was influenced by that interesting man Sir Geoffrey Vickers, who served with courage in the stupidity, mud and blood of the First World War, for which he received both British and French gallantry medals. Sir Geoffrey's war experience showed him the need for better ways of organising complex matters of supplies and transport, but also impressed on him the importance of human qualities such as courage, loyalty, and commitment. After that war he returned to university to study law, but he also pondered the application of mathematics to large scale planning, military or otherwise. In the Second World War, as already mentioned, he developed the useful area of study now known as Operations Research. As a good thinker, he well understood that the best of logical plans can fail if human nature and behaviour are ignored.

Due to some characteristics of human nature, especially pride, dishonesty, cunning, and ambition, key searching disputes will sometimes arise between scientists, or sometimes between scientists and those who choose to wander further from the lamp post; and even sometimes between those bold wanderers in the gloom. There will be shouts of *the keys are here*, and *no they're not, they are over here*, or *you've got the wrong keys*. Is there some way to resolve such disputes, when some of the searchers may be in no fit state to know whether they have the right keys or not?

Peter Checkland has creatively extended Geoffrey Vicker's work, under the title of Soft Systems Analysis. It is to Peter that I owe the term *rich pictures*, which, in his refreshing style, he also calls *fried egg and string* models. I think his ideas can help to sort out contradictory views on bushfire management. His rich pictures can include both the areas under the lamp posts, and further afield. They can creatively help to discover more than one set of keys, and identify the ones relevant to the task in hand. Importantly, they recognise the importance of human emotion and opinion. You will find some examples of rich pictures on the World Wide Web. They are deceptively childlike, but can challenge, and help, the best of minds. Importantly, they are capable of evolving, as our understanding increases.

I hope Peter Checkland will not be offended if I call him a philosopher, and suggest that his rich pictures are useful tools for a philosophy of Australian bushfire management, exploring the relationships within and between people, landscape, and complex bushfire behaviour. I hope Mary Midgley and Geoffrey Vickers, were they still alive, would agree. An initiative in Australia might be beneficial to other fire prone lands, such as California, Canada, Africa, and southern Europe. On the other hand, we could, as has happened in other matters, just leave it to other nations, and stumble along behind.

The Australian bushfire problem definitely has cross-disciplinary philosophical aspects. It certainly involves physics, chemistry, and biology, but also politics, law, psychology, economics, history, and Aboriginal knowledge. I think the ideas discussed above can help us get our bushfire policy straight, before we waste further billions of dollars on trying to control uncontrollable mega-fires, instead of taking common sense action to avoid them.

Above all, we must beware of attention seeking supposed '*bushfire experts*', without practical fire experience, but with impressive academic titles, achieved through luxuriant lists of publications, sometimes achieved by long lists of joint papers. If uncritically believed, such publications may lead us into even worse strife.

Mary Midgely once commented on the nonsensical administrative idea of judging a scientist's worth simply by the number of papers, or even pages published, without regard to their quality. She foresaw future historians being amazed at such administrative naivety. Perhaps I am an historian, because I have been amazed for some time.

-oOo-

Essay 4

Pines, Pigs & a Pinch of Salt

'No lesson seems to be so deeply inculcated by the experience of life as that you never should trust experts.'
Lord Salisbury, letter to Lord Lytton, 1877.

The entertaining, or depressing, circus of good Australian public money being spent on local, or assorted overseas experts, is not as new as some may think. In 1914 the West Australian Government invited a then much acclaimed British forester, Sir David E. Hutchins, to visit and advise them on forest policy. Hutchins was a graduate of the famous *École Nationale des Eaux et des Forêts* at Nancy, in France.

According to fire historian Professor Stephen Pyne of Arizona, this establishment was run on the lines of a military academy, with students wearing cloaks and carrying swords. On graduation, French students were commissioned into the army. After his graduation, Hutchins spent some years as a British colonial forest superintendent in India and South Africa, with or without a sword. In 1914 he made his first visit to Australia.

To Hutchins' eye, the *jarrah* forest of Western Australia was *'half-empty'*, and frequent bushfires were a major obstacle to timber production. He had obviously been informed, and wrote that, the *jarrah* forest was, in those days, traditionally burnt on average every three years. Other evidence, offered in later essays, suggests it must have been so for a very long time, by the indigenous *Noongar* people. This frequent, mild, patchy burning prevented serious fires developing, and played an important role in the germination of seeds, and the stimulation of grass and other plants for kangaroos, and other animals. Frequent fire promoted some food and medicine plants used by *Noongar* folk, and ensured that most fires were mild and, importantly for nature conservation, patchy.

On the basis of his French education, Hutchins regarded himself as a

15

forest scientist, and had been indoctrinated by the then current forestry ideas from France, British India, and South Africa, with the idea that fire was *'the forester's enemy'*. He felt his duty was to put a complete stop to it. Part of his master plan was to underplant the *jarrah* forest with pine trees. These would be planted in strips, in the belief that they would spread through the whole forest by self-sown seeds. He regarded this as *'a sacred duty to posterity'*. In his opinion, once the *jarrah* forest was *'filled up'* with pines it would be so shady as to be fireproof. This may rather surprise those of us who have seen pine trees explode in flames on a hot Australian summer day. They produce a fireball much like a napalm bomb.

But the sacred duty continued. These shady pine trees were to be the basis of a lucrative turpentine industry, using the labour of sturdy migrants. Hutchins recommended the peasants of the French region called the *Landes*. These migrants would run vast herds of goats and swine in the forest, feeding them on acorns from oaks, which would be planted amongst the pines. Cattle grazing in the forest would *'do no harm, and often much good in helping to brush off the side branches and keep the soil clean against forest fires.'*

Hutchins had a bold vision for Australian tourism. This *jarrah*-pine-oak forest was to be stocked with herds of deer, wild boar, *mouflon*, pheasants and partridges, so attracting wealthy English tourists on shooting holidays, to be organised by the travel agent Thomas Cook. These *'valuable game animals'* would be protected by foresters, who would allow them *'to gradually run wild where conditions are favourable, and to keep a hand on them afterwards against poachers.'* Perhaps his quasi-military education showed when he declared that foresters *'should be armed and be soldiers of the State ... In South Africa foresters are given arms and ammunition'*.

One reason for his opposition to forest fire becomes clear. The armed foresters were to get rid of vermin, *'as it is got rid of in England; and with the control of vermin and forest fires, game introduction will at last become a success in Australian forests.'* Indeed, sportsmen had told him that *'bushfires have had most to do with the failure of partridge, pheasants and other game in Australian forests; more, in fact, than vermin'*. Perhaps this is the reasoning behind his later proposal to introduce polecats, weasels and stoats to control the rabbits.

Having solved the problems of the *jarrah* forest, our eminent consultant then turned his orderly and penetrating mind to the *karri* forest, further south. Those of us who have fought raging fires in tall *karri* forest, will be interested to hear that, according to Hutchins, *'The karri forest in its natural condition does not burn...'*. He regarded the *karri* forest, like the *jarrah*, as half-empty, and suggested that the *'stream sides and swamps in the karri forest should be filled up with blackwood'*. Blackwood is a shrub from eastern Australia. It forms thickets, which burn very fiercely. He seems to have overlooked the outstanding commercial potential of the *karri* forest for growing blackberries and *marijuana*.

Hutchins had trenchant views on the training of foresters. He noted that *'it is a common notion in Australia that forestry and botany are the same.'* While he accepted that foresters needed to know a few tree species, *'At best, ordinary botany is an interesting pursuit for the forester's leisure hours; on the whole not so useful as photography, or meteorology.'* The two chief qualifications needed by a forester were *'administrative ability and skill in making forest working-plans'*. Might I dare to suggest that he overlooked the potential benefits of philosophy in a forester's education?

The term *'eminent forest consultant'* has an impressive ring to it, and Hutchins' ideas, particularly on fire exclusion, were widely implemented between 1920 and 1961. The result was uncontrollable fires in the heavy scrub and litter accumulation. The rapid spread of the fires was due mainly to wind, which was sometimes caused by convection from the fires themselves. The intense convection of the fires was due to heavy leaf litter, sticks, bark, capsules, and scrub, the legacy of a neglect of frequent burning.

Such heavy litter has exacerbated the recent effects of drought, and extended fire seasons. Some blame these on increased atmospheric CO_2, others on El Niño, or the Indian Ocean Dipole, others on the interaction between the Solar Wind and the Earth's magnetic field. I am not in a position to judge, and am wary of people who promote themselves as experts on the matter. Despite the attractive rhetorical alliteration, I don't think the science is yet settled, and it may never be. This thought should open a cheerful vista for those academics who rely on government grants in climate science, and good luck to them, as long as they don't lead us up a dangerous garden path.

I believe some Aboriginal Elders are real experts on bushfire, due to thousands of years of cumulative practical experience. With exceptions such as rainforest, most Australian grassland, heath, scrub, or forest, needs to be deliberately patch burnt, regularly, to recycle nutrients, maintain diversity, protect small unburnt refuges for animals, and prevent monster wildfires. Sir David Hutchins' expert opinions on bushfire were dangerous, muddle headed, management advice. They should, as they possibly said at Nancy, be taken *'avec un petit grain de sel'* (with a little grain of salt).

After his short visit to Australia, Sir David moved on to New Zealand, where he gave that government valuable advice on the importation and use of elephants in forestry. Possibly he published a refereed scientific paper, or government report, on this matter, and added it to his *curriculum vitae*.

-oOo-

Essay 5

*Noongar*s Knew Best

'On our way we met a party of natives engaged in burning the bush, which they do in sections every year. The dexterity with which they manage so proverbially a dangerous agent as fire is indeed astonishing. Those to whom this duty is especially entrusted, and who guide or stop the running flame, are armed with large green boughs, with which, if it moves in a wrong direction, they beat it out. ... I can conceive no finer subject for a picture than a party of these swarthy beings engaged in kindling, moderating, and directing the destructive element, which under their care seems almost to change its nature, acquiring, as it were, complete docility, instead of the ungovernable fury we are accustomed to ascribe to it.'

Commander John Lort Stokes R.N. observing Noongar burning just north of Albany, between 2nd and 15th November, 1840.
Discoveries in Australia, Voyage of HMS Beagle 1837-1843.
(By courtesy of Gutenberg Press)

Much has been written, some as scientific papers, some as newspaper or magazine articles, some as Facebook posts, about the supposed irreparable harm done to plants and animals by deliberate burning to reduce fuels in south-west Australia. Claims have been made, and taken seriously in some quarters, that burning at intervals less than the time taken to flower and produce seed will unfailingly exterminate plant species.

Those who have observed many bushfires in south-western Australia have known, for a long time, that frequent burning, in light fuel, produces subsequent brilliant wildflowers, green healthy bush, and, importantly, a mosaic of burnt and unburnt patches. In light fuel, on a cool day, even the shadow from a bush can create an unburnt patch. It has also been shown, by experiment, that frequent burning in light fuels does indeed produce patchy fires. Some patches may not burn for long periods, perhaps never.

So a long term seedbank can be maintained, although in some places, long fire exclusion itself may lead to seed loss by rot, or insect attack. At the same time, only a tiny percentage of native plants in *jarrah* forest need long intervals between fires, and these occur in obvious fire shelters, such as moist creek banks and amongst rocks. According to Dr. Neil Burrows, an eminent West Australian forester, the overwhelming majority of shrub and herb plant species in the *jarrah* forest flower within three to four years, which is rather interesting, in view of many historical reports of burning at such intervals.

Near the south coast of Western Australia, a species of *Banksia*, previously described as fire sensitive, was found to actually increase four fold under burning at 2-3 year intervals, despite needing 4 years to flower and produce seed. Such an apparent paradox shows that ecology is complex, and what passes as ecology, and appears as wordy papers in refereed journals, is sometimes misleading, being based on simplistic, sometimes false, or sometimes overlooked assumptions.

Medieval Scottish lawyers coined the excellent word *subreption* to describe evidence in a court of law which misleads, not by lying, but by omitting part of the truth. In trying to use logic in ecology, we might cautiously remember Ambrose Bierce's deep philosophical definition of logic (1911) as *'the art of thinking and reasoning in strict accordance with the limitations and incapacities of the human misunderstanding'* (Essay 15). His suspicions were not new. Much earlier, the French philosophers Michel de Montaigne (1533-1592) and Voltaire (1694-1778) both suggested that a simplistic obsession with logic is a sure sign of stupidity.

Supposed landscape logic can play tricks, and should be cross checked with the humanity of history. An important historical basis of the truth about landscape fire in south-west Australia is that before Europeans arrived, *Noongar* people managed the south-west Australian dry forests and woodlands very well without the self-important, yet simplistic findings of some academic biologists, and without the quasi-military fire suppression efforts of thousands of fire fighters, using fire trucks, water bombers and helicopters; and without the involvement of sensation seeking television journalists, pretentious politicians, the Conservation Council, the Conservation Commission, the Wilderness Society, the WA Forest Alliance, the Minister for Emergency Services, the Department of Fire and Emergency Services (DFES), the Minister for the Environment, the Department of Biodiversity, Conservation and Attractions (DBCA), the Department of Water and Environmental Resources (DWER), and not forgetting the Salvation Army to give them all breakfast. Seventy years ago, before the days of management science, my mother told me that *'too many cooks spoil the broth'.*

Noongars managed fire very simply, albeit based on deep historical knowledge, by burning frequently, in most places as often as the leaf litter would carry a mild, creeping fire, as described by Commander John Stokes. In the *jarrah* forest, this is every 3-4 years, that is to say, in the fire season between the third and fourth winter after the last fire. Some of us know, from practical experience, that within the *jarrah* forest, patches of *marri* litter will carry a fire every 2-3 years, and some *coondli* (sheoak) groves every year.

Historical evidence (Essay 6) shows, beyond any reasonable doubt, that much *Noongar* burning in *jarrah-marri forest* was in summer, which can only be safely done in light, patchy fuels, 2-4 years old. In the *wandoo* forest, formerly with a grassy floor, it was every 2-3 years. *Wandoo* germinates best on ash beds. Archaeological evidence from *balga* grasstree stems shows 2-4 year burning also in *Banksia* woodland north of Perth, and the same in *tuart* forest. I have been told that there was even some burning in winter, for example on the south coast of Western Australia, where certain sedges will carry fire over standing water. I return to this interesting matter later (Essay 21).

Frequent, patchy, burning maintained a high diversity of habitats, and so a high diversity of plants and animals, some of which were food or medicine for *Noongars*. As John Stokes described, they used green branches to swat out fires heading for places they did not want to burn. These included spear shaft thickets, which, according to a late *Noongar* Elder, needed twelve years to reach a useful length. Twelve is, of course, three times four or four times three. *Noongars* walked near late spring or summer fires in little clothing, including bare feet, so, quite obviously, bushfires were much milder in those days than now, when fuels are heavier, and expensive protective boots, goggles, gloves, helmets and clothing are essential. This might not occur to, say, a botanist with no practical experience of bushfire.

Some claim that recent fierce fires are due to hotter summers, but some of our hottest recent bushfires have happened on quite mild days, with ambient air temperature of only about 25 degrees Celsius. The main difference between a century ago and now is that litter has been allowed to pile up for decades. A lot more fuel means much hotter fires, regardless of climate vagaries. Anyone who does not believe that has clearly not faced a bushfire, and felt the obviously differing radiant heat between light and heavy fuels, and noted the tendency of heavy fuel to produce a stronger convection column, more flying embers, and so faster rate of fire spread. In such fires, water bombers can be of little use. From the ground, I have seen the water they drop evaporate, or be wafted upward by the strong convection. General exclusion of fire for decades, as urged by some self styled *'fire experts'* leads to fires that roar rather than crackle, and can even cause the ground to shake. Burning balls of gas, as big as a house, can break free from the fire front, and roll across bare paddocks. Those of us who have actually fought such fires would rather not be exposed to them.

Even in areas little used by *Noongars*, most of the bush would have burnt frequently by mild and unimpeded summer lightning fires, trickling on for months, flaring in some places which had missed the previous fire, reducing fuel, raising soil pH, stimulating soil bacteria, and recycling nutrients. Such mild fires, sometimes large in area, sometimes small, continued up to the 1920s, before there were many Bushfire Brigades, and before the Forests Department had developed long range fire fighting capacity. Spreading at a conservative one kilometre a day, a fire starting in spring could travel more than a hundred kilometres over the fire season, before autumn rain doused it. They would most likely have gone out sooner, due to running into a recently burnt area. Much of the landscape would have burnt as often as it could carry a trickling fire, and this created and maintained mosaics at various scales, so preventing the ferocious fires we see today. Attempted long and widespread fire exclusion in south-west Australia is a new fangled notion, poor ecology, and unintelligent fire management.

Frequent fire made the bush safe for *Noongars*, and promoted grass for *yonka* (kangaroo), and a host of bush tucker plants. It produced *byoo*, the red fruit of the *djiridji (*zamia), an important *Noongar* food. Frequent light smoke germinated seeds, maintained large areas of grass, and provoked flowering of kangaroo paws and *balga* grasstrees. Native grasses, kangaroo paws and *byoo* are increasingly rare, under an advocacy which claims that we should exclude fire from large bush areas for decades.

This foolish idea makes the bush very dangerous, as we have seen in many recent fierce bushfires. Unless political common sense prevails in bushfire policy, there will, no doubt, be more uncontrollable bushfires, property loss, and, inevitably, loss of human life. We don't need any more incredibly expensive public enquiries into bushfire to establish that fact. Nor do we need any more half-baked advice on fire contributed by those with little or no direct experience of it.

There is a fallacious claim that, left alone, the litter will all rot down to enrich the soil with humus, as it does in temperate climates, or rainforests. The truth in south-west Australia, as any observant bush worker or resident will testify, is that there is slight decay in winter, but the summer blizzard of dead leaves, bark, twigs and seed capsules is far greater, so litter builds up fast. After twenty years or so, there is a mulching effect, and the increase slows down. However, by then most native plants are smothered, discoloured, and straggly, most of the nutrient is locked up in dead matter,

21

and the soil under the litter is increasingly acid. Frequent, mild fire releases the nutrients, sweetens the soil, prunes some plants, and germinates the seeds of others.

For decades, a small but vociferous group in south-west Australia has opposed prescribed burning. Part of the battle goes on in what is called '*refereed literature*', another part in the news media, through press releases, and yet more on social media, such as Facebook. However, standards of refereeing and editorial wisdom are variable, and I'm sure I do not need to warn readers to apply caution to Facebook posts.

There are some reliable historical references on frequent, widespread burning by *Noongars*. In her excellent book '*Fire & Hearth*', the late Dr Sylvia Hallam noted that in 1837 Lt. Henry Bunbury, who had travelled down the west coastal plain, mentioned '*...the periodical extensive bush fires which, by destroying every two to three years the dead leaves, plants, sticks, fallen timber etc. prevent most effectually the accumulation of any decayed vegetable deposit... being the last month of summer ... the Natives have burnt with fire much of the country...*'.

Bunbury was from an English farming family, and his view of *Noongar* burning was probably based on a belief that humus is essential to all plants. Yet, in some systems, humus can be replaced by charcoal as storage for nutrients and bacteria. This is now recognised by a body of soil scientists, who recommend the addition of *biochar* to soils.

Dr Ian Abbott, a former Principal Research Scientist with the then Department of Conservation and Land Management, has reported that in 1975 Mr Frank Thompson was interviewed about his memories of fire near the south coast, before the First World War. He said '*You see, the Natives ...they used to burn the country every three or four years...when it was burnt the grass grew and it was nice and fresh and the possums had something to live on and the kangaroos had something to live on and the wallabies and the tamars and boodie rat ...It didn't burn very fast because it was only grass and a few leaves here and there and it would burn ahead and...sometimes there'd be a little isolated patch of other stuff that wasn't good enough to burn the time before, but as it burnt along perhaps there might be some wallabies or tamars ...those animals didn't run away from fire, they'd run up to it and you'd see them hopping along the edge of the fire until they saw a place where the fire wasn't burning very fierce...*'.

It is hard to imagine wallabies or *boodie* rats hopping along the flame front of recent bushfires, looking for a way through. Long fire exclusion is causing atrocious bushfires, and many avoidable wildlife deaths. Larger animals, such as emus and kangaroos, cannot escape fires, due to the dense litter, sticks, and undergrowth. Small animals, such as *goomal* (possums), burn their feet off, by running on embers. Soil seedbanks can be destroyed. The longer fire has been excluded, the fewer the unburnt refuges left when

22

it does occur, and the longer the bush takes to recover after a fire. Where large, mature trees are killed outright, as has happened in several recent fires in heavy fuel, it will take hundreds of years for them to be replaced. Oddly, those who oppose fuel reduction burning are often the same ones who claim to be protectors of the forest.

Under frequent, light burning, there would have been thousands of small refuges, in rocks or near creeks, which would have burnt less often, some never. Recent fierce fires destroy these, and the fire sensitive plants and animals they formerly protected. The advocacy of long fire exclusion over large areas obtusely ignores the refuges of the very plants and animals it claims to care for.

Fire marks on old *balga* grasstree stems show clearly that, in some places, two to four year burning only continued widely until the First World War or soon after. In others, it continued up to the 1930s, and even the 1950s. Some old settler families in the Perth Hills remember when any fire in *jarrah* forest could be put out with wet bags or green branches. This is generally only possible when fires are in litter no more than four years old, with flames less than a metre high. *Noongars* knew, and still know that, and helpfully passed that knowledge on to early European settlers. It seems to have been lost in our urban intellectual wilderness.

Far from destroying diversity, this frequent burning enhanced it.. Animals had both food and shelter, and wildflowers flourished. Today's blanket fire exclusion in National Parks leads to an eventual single, blanket, fierce fire, which simplifies the ecosystem down to a single age. It also destroys that part of the seed bank suspended within the leaf litter.

As an example, this is the likely outcome for Yalgorup National Park, on the Indian Ocean coast of south-western Australia, formerly burnt at short intervals by *Noongars* and early graziers. There has been little or no controlled burning since 1960, when grazing leases expired, and the park was established. When a severe fire eventually happens, most of the remaining *tuart* trees will be killed outright, as will many equally old grasstrees. In my view, that park is now a death trap in summer, since peppermint trees, greatly increased since burning ceased, burn like napalm. Last time I was there, there were few turn around points on the sandy tracks, on which one can easily become bogged, and potentially killed.

By pointing out to our political representatives, that the DBCA should be adequately funded to burn National Parks at short intervals, and hence more lightly and patchily, and that the Department of Fire and Emergency Services should be funded to burn the bush around human settlements more often, so creating defensive fine grained mosaics, we will make human life safer, see more wildflowers, have healthier forests, reduce animal deaths, and avoid dense, choking smoke from fierce wildfires. We will have to live with occasional light smoke from controlled burns.

If most litter were less than five years old, smoke would be minimal, and arson futile. All it could cause would be a mild, creeping fire, with occasional small flare ups, which would benefit the bush. Patchy fire refuges would be protected. As a former forest workman, I know that magpies love a mild, creeping fire, in light fuel. They stand around it and snaffle the hundreds of spiders and cockroaches that run out, making an audible rustling noise, probably unknown in the groves of academe. I have never seen a magpie near a big, fierce fire. They are intelligent birds. Perhaps an intelligent ornithologist would like to study their behaviour in the presence of different kinds of fire.

Think of the savings and benefits by working with nature, instead of fighting it. Recent bushfires in heavy fuel have cost tens of millions of dollars. Using *Noongar* fire knowledge and practice, there need, eventually, be no more squadrons of very expensive, taxpayer funded aircraft, anxious home owners, and dense, choking smoke for a week or more.

Given current suburban housing, there will always be a need for fire brigades and their equipment. However, more young *Noongar* people, and others, could be employed by the DBCA to help manage the National Parks and reserves with fire. This would maintain forest health, and restore *Noongar* culture. Those people who live close to National Parks would have some peace of mind in summer. If, as some claim, summers will soon get catastrophically hotter, then the argument for more frequent burning is even stronger.

A few years ago, in a submission to the inquiry into the Waroona/Yarloop fire (2016), I suggested that *Noongar* Elders should be drawn into discussions, with a view to creating more intelligent bushfire policy. I got no reply, and don't know if such discussions were held, but I'm sure they will eventually.

In his report on the Waroona/Yarloop fire, Euan Ferguson AFSM discussed bushfire policies. Good policies will only arise from good philosophy. We must ask the philosophical question, shall bushfire be our enemy, or our friend? *Noongar* people asked and answered that question, intelligently, thousands of years ago. There are some people in our present society, even in universities, to whom that philosophical question has seemingly not occurred. Even when it is spelt out, some academics do not understand it. Those in a first class carriage aboard the fire ecology research funding gravy train may not want to understand it.

-oOo-

Essay 6

Bushfire Truth in Old Letters

> *'No arts; no letters; no society...'*
> Thomas Hobbes, *Leviathan, 1651*

Trying to set the historical record of bushfire straight, I transcribed some interesting old letters from the original handwriting on microfilm at the Battye Library. These letters now reside at the State Records Office of Western Australia, Consignment 36, Volume 152, folios 49-63. I am most grateful to the Battye Library for the original access, and to the State Records Office for permission to use these letters.

I was put on the trail of this correspondence by the late Dr Sylvia Hallam, mentioned before as the author of 'Fire & Hearth', a fascinating, and I believe truthful book about *Noongar* people, including their traditional use of fire in south-west Australia.

Before any scholars object to my spelling of '*honor*', I must point out that such spelling was consistent in the letters, and seems to have been the accepted spelling then amongst British folk. How sensible they were.

These letters are part of the undeniable cross-disciplinary evidence that *Noongar* people did traditionally manage the bush by burning, and that fire was generally much more frequent before European arrival than since. Oddly, some academics claim it was the other way round. It will be interesting to see how they explain the following letters.

The first letter, in 1846, is from the newly appointed Governor of Western Australia, Colonel Andrew Clarke. The settlers at York had complained of *Noongar* fires destroying their crops and grazing. As a new arrival from Britain, Governor Clarke sought advice from his magistrates, and other senior officials.

Letter 1

The Governor clearly did not realise that making fires less frequent would also make them fiercer when they did occur. An alarming number of people today wear the same blinkers.

Circular 17 February 1846
Residents and Protectors of Natives

Sir

His Excellency the Governor having heard with much regret of the serious damage and loss of property which the settlers, especially in the York District and the past season, have sustained by fires made either or otherwise by the natives, is very desirous of adopting some measure which would, if it did not entirely put a stop to these fires, at all events have the effect of making them less frequent.

With this view His Excellency wishes you to consider the subject and offer such suggestions thereupon as your experience may dictate.
I have the honor to be … (Signature missing on microfilm, but Peter Broun was Secretary at that time.)

Letter 2

The first to reply was Richard Bland, who gave a balanced view of *Noongar* burning. He saw no malicious intent in their custom.

York March 2nd 1846

Sir

I have the honor to acknowledge receipt of your circular of 17th February on the subject of Bush Fires, and wishing any suggestions with a view to their prevention for the future.

I fear His Excellency will find it a very difficult subject to deal with, and impossible wholly to prevent, it has always been the custom of the Natives to fire the country during the summer season for a variety of purposes, first to assist them in hunting, it also clears the country of underwood, which if not occasionally burnt, would become an impenetrable jungle, infested with snakes and reptiles.

The principal fires in this District that occurred during the earlier part of the present season, originated either from the Settlers themselves, or from the Natives setting fire to hollow trees to dislodge the opossum. December and January being their principal season for hunting them, they have never been accustomed, and are unable in most cases if they wished, to put the fires out, and when the tree falls, the grass ignites and is so extremely dry that the fire will run for many miles, until either a road or some bare spot checks its progress. The principal fire at the Toodyay where three fields of wheat were burnt, originated from a Settler burning a tree near his house.

I consider it an advantage that portions of the country should be burnt every year, provided it is not done till late in the summer, the feed is always better where the dead grass has been previously burnt off.

When I first settled in the District, and got acquainted with the Natives, finding myself much inconvenienced by the bush fires, I commenced the practice of giving them presents of flour and clothing when the first rains set in, provided they had not fired the country during the summer, I found this plan succeed [sic] *to a certain extent, and it was followed up by the Government, who through me used to give them presents until two or three years since, when it was discontinued I believe for want of funds.*

I have made every enquiry in the District both personally, and through the Police, as to the origin of the fires this season, and do not think that in any one instance they have originated through any malicious intent, the evil however requires some remedy, as the law at present only applies to cases of burning crops of corn, stacks, buildings etc.

It would be hard to debar the Native the food Providence has placed at his disposal, by preventing the use of Fire, without which he cannot procure it. I have no doubt a great deal may be done by rewarding them with Flour and Clothing, to induce them to give up this practice until later in the season, and by passing an act of Council to punish them, when they can be proved to have done it with a decided intent to injure the Settler, and also to prevent the Settlers themselves from making fires for clearing, or other purposes, until the corn has been all harvested.

I have the Honor to be, Sir,
Your Obedient Servant
R.H. Bland
Protector of Natives

Letter 3

The next respondent was a former British army officer, and Waterloo veteran, Captain Richard Meares. He took a more authoritarian and colonial view.

York, March 3rd 1846

Sir

In reverting to your letter of the 17th. February Inst. wherein His Excellency the Governor expresses a wish that I should consider the subject of the Natives firing the bush and to offer any suggestion which might be adopted to prevent the occurrence – even in part – of the very serious damage sustained in the York District by this practice. It seems necessary to premise in the first instance that when this Territory was taken from the Aborigines and by Act of Parliament they were created British Subjects – 'no equivalent for them having been reserved' – it would appear the intention was that they should still maintain themselves as in their primitive state – if so - they burn for their food – whereas the existence of our Flocks and Herds depends on what to us is thus annually irretrievably destroyed and the whole district is now groaning under the ruinous spoliation: some impute it to the Squatting Act which has of late caused a new occupation and thus as it were driven them from their second resource – the first being the old settled Districts. Here are three parties, the Government, the Natives, and the Settlers: the Government let to A.B. [Anybody?] 4000 acres of land for one year having previously paid ten pounds for a license, the next day the whole of these Lands are fired and burned bare by the Natives: the Lambing has commenced, the sheep die, and the farmer is ruined: now it would certainly appear that these lands should be protected by the Government itself – but hitherto the battle has been fought by the new owners against the old ones. The Settlers have adopted a custom of giving at Harvest Time, from each farm, one bushel of wheat to each Tribe 'provided they do not burn the run' as also gleaning of the fields, to both which advantages they are [reckless or feckless?]; and on this ground we at present stand.

Now it strikes me that whatever is done for these people should come through some higher Authority than the owner of each farm – the proprietors might give in their quota in kind to be deposited for distribution in the hands of a proper officer of the Government who I should say were equally bound with the Settlers to pay in a bountiful [mite?]: all the Tribes have their Chiefs although I believe not very commanding ones but still they might be selected, encouraged, and made very useful in holding control over the rest by investing them with authority to receive from the Government officer and distribute although in the officer's presence and to distinguish them with some mark of favour – if they deserved it – some pains might be taken to educate each Chief in our language so that they might become interpreters and know and understand amongst themselves gradually as the light may break in upon them that we are trying to render them ultimate service and which Time will teach them to appreciate. If we are to keep Flocks it is quite clear that the Lands must be preserved and not fired: and thus the immediate attention of the Natives should be called to the subject, to warn them against solitary confinement and Rottnest [A penal island off the West Australian coast], *and that for the future, in no one instance will firing the country be overlooked for they laugh at our idea of letting a fire escape them if they wish to put it out, and the wheat collected would I should imagine be more than equivalent to what they would otherwise obtain by those burnings and would also come at the very period when they perform their destructive operations being in January and February.*

If I have written my opinions rather freely I beg to assure His Excellency they are the thoughts of an Old Settler who has the prosperity of the Colony most dearly at heart.

I have the Honor to be Sir
Your most obedient Humble Servant
Richard G. Meares, Resident

Letter 4

Charles Symmons was sympathetic to the *Noongars*, and recognised some of their reasons for burning. However, like the Governor, he did not foresee that less frequent burning would, inevitably, lead to fiercer fires. He suggested an even handed approach, with penalties for settlers too if they caused damage by fire.

Perth March 3rd. 1846

Sir

I have the honor to acknowledge the receipt of your letter dated the 17th. of February Inst., expressive of His Excellency's wish that I might endeavour to suggest some measures for the putting a stop to the fires kindled in the bush by the Natives, or at least rendering them of less frequent occurrence.

In reply, I must first beg leave to draw His Excellency's attention to the fact that although by far the larger proportion of bush-fires are occasioned by the Natives, yet that many originate in the wilful or careless conduct of the Settlers themselves. The smouldering ashes of a woodcutter's fire – the chance spark from his pipe are all sufficient means of combustion amongst vegetation parched to tinder by the summer heat. I merely allude to these facts to show the necessity of making some restrictive enactments for the white man as well as for the black.

As regards the Aborigines, I need scarcely point out to His Excellency, that, as in all cases connected with an interference in native habits and feelings – the question of the best means of remedy is one of considerable difficulty.

My knowledge of the Native character renders me extremely sceptical as to the success of any remedial plan for checking one of their most ancient and cherished privileges – but, as in all my transactions with this singular people, I have never been discouraged by the failure of measures which must in the first instance be purely experimental – so, in this case – let some plan of operation be devised – and should it fail – we can only recommence de novo.

I should suggest therefore to His Excellency the practicability of informing the Natives in all the settled Districts of the determination henceforward of the Government to put a stop to their custom of indiscriminately firing the bush, and that on no pretence whatever are they to commence their burning operations before the beginning of the month of March – after which period they may be allowed to do so – the immediate vicinity of the Settlers' homesteads being rigidly excepted. That, provided such regulations be observed on the part of the Natives, the Settlers and the Government combined, should undertake on the 1st. of March of each year to distribute in their several districts through means of the Protectors and the Resident Magistrates, such gratuities of flour as may at once suffice the cupidity of the Natives and convince them of the policy of compliance with our regulations.

I consider this plan as at least worthy of consideration (however much it may be modified or enlarged) it having been found effectual in the neighborhood of some farms in the York District, where the Shepherds confirm that by this gratuity they could calculate with tolerable certainty on the period for the native firing of the bush.

It will be for the Law Officers of the Crown to determine as to the nature and extent of the penalty to be enforced on the infringement of any arrangements of this nature which may be entered on between the Aborigines and the Government.

I must, in conclusion beg to recall to the attention of His Excellency the equal necessity of legislative restriction in the case of the Settlers and their farm laborers.

I have the honor to be Sir,
Yr very Obedient Servt
Chas Symmons, Protector of Natives

Letter 5

Lt. Col. John Molloy was an early settler in what is now called the Busselton area. In those days it was well occupied by *Noongar* people called *Wadandi*, whose descendants still live there. They used fire to hunt and manage the bush, and Molloy partly understood this. His wife, Georgiana, possibly had an even better understanding of fire. She collected the seeds of wild plants to send to England, and, in a letter, mentioned the importance of burning. Her husband's letter is below.

Vasse 17th March 1846

Sir

I have to acknowledge the receipt of the circular of the 17th. Ult. In reference to its contents I must confess my utter inability to offer an opinion as to any effective means of controlling the incendiary propensities of the Natives. Speaking of this district I should say we have not suffered any great inconvenience from Bushfires, the Natives carefully abstaining from their practice until after the harvest is fully accomplished an event to which they look forward with a degree of pleasurable anxiety.

A stern command not to destroy the pasturage with a threat of banishment from the habitations of the Settlers has its effect and so far from Bush fires being generally offensive I believe the opinion prevails in this quarter that they are not only necessary but salubrious.

There are doubtless measures of prevention capable of adoption such as individuals taking the initiative in burning when the country is not in a forward combustible state and the fires can be easily arrested, perhaps they would require encouragement to effect the formation of a barrier belt around points requiring protection.

Finally the prospect of Reward by holding out to the Natives the enjoyment of a General Corrobory throughout the district when the distribution of about three pounds of flour to each native on a named day might be offered to them provided a proper degree of abstinence [illegible] *should have been observed this would not as far as I can be permitted to form an estimate be a consideration to the proprietors but of a trifling nature.*

I have the honor to be Sir
Your most Obedt. Servant
J. Molloy
Resd. Magistrate

Letter 6

Francis Singleton described two year burning on the then grassy coastal plain around Dandalup. Like Charles Symmons, he was aware of some of the *Noongar* reasons for burning.

Dandalup March 7 1846

Sir

I have the honor to acknowledge the receipt of your circular concerning the damage sustained by the Settlers through the means of Bush Fires; and requesting me to forward for the information of His Excellency such suggestions as might present themselves to my mind.

In reply to the same I would first observe that my experience of the evil alluded to has been confined to this District, which is of a character totally different to that of the Districts eastward of the Range.

In those parts of the Territory a Bush fire will, as has been proved during this season, extend for many miles, not only burning up all vegetation and thereby causing severe damage to the flocks and herds, but utterly destroying the property of several of the Settlers.

In this District it is quite otherwise – the major part of the country to the Westwd [sic] of the range being sandy these districts are only partially burnt, and as a general rule I would remark that the vegetation will only burn once in two years – Further; it appears to be about one half of the sandy land burns over by the fires annually; the graziers are therefore fortunately secure in having the other portion for the sustenance of their flocks and herds. The herbage, unless it has been burnt in the previous summer becomes exceedingly hard, and is usually refused by the stock – The fires are never general and if not intentionally lighted by the Europeans for the purpose mentioned, are kindled by the Natives for the purpose of more effectually securing their game; which is captured in extraordinary numbers where a strong wind impels the flames.

I think I may with safety say, that since I have resided in this district no damage has occurred from Bush fires where common precaution has been made use of to prevent the calamities supposed to attend a fire of that nature

… [A lengthy discussion of domestic fires, smoking, and the law has been omitted]

To frame a statute forbidding the Natives to fire the bush would I fancy prove abortive; and could such a law be carried out in practice I should conceive it to be an unjust one. The Aborigines look forward to the summer season with the same feelings as Europeans – To both it is the time of harvest – It is then that they gather in by means of these fires their great harvests of game; and altho' [sic] in many districts they have been bribed (or paid) for not setting fire to the bush, I look upon it as unjust to demand them to abstain from securing their game or their means of subsistence in a manner which they find to be the most effective.

As well might we compel them to desist from smoking opossums out of trees, on the grounds of such a practice injuring our timber, as to enforce the former rule because our sheep lack feed.

[The last few paragraphs mainly discuss feed for sheep, and have been omitted.]

I have the honor to be Sir
Your obed. Srvt.
Francis Corbet Singleton
Resident

Letter 7

George Eliot seems to have had good, if paternalistic, relations with the *Noongar* people around Bunbury. Like Lt. Col. Molloy, he was aware of some of their reasons for burning, and approved of them.

Resident's Office, Bunbury, March 9th 1846

Sir

I beg to acknowledge the receipt of a Circular from your Office of the 17th Ulto requesting me to offer any suggestion experience may dictate on the subject of the prevention of fires made accidentally or otherwise by the Natives in the Bush.

In answer thereto I beg to state that the only means I am aware of for that purpose would be for the Government to offer a Reward to be given at the commencement of the Rainy Season to the Natives of the districts that have been least burnt. Such a measure would probably partially prevent burning the Country and would also perhaps induce the Natives to stop those fires that come from a distance. At the same time I must observe that in my opinion every Settler ought at the beginning of the dry season to burn a strip of country in the immediate neighbourhood of his homestead by these means he would be perfectly secure from Bush Fires and by merely giving up a day or two's work probably save his property from destruction.

I am not myself at all adverse to the practice of burning the Country inasmuch as it produces better food for the stock and also destroys an enormous number of Reptiles and Insects which would in a few years were it not for the fires increase to such a degree as to render the country almost uninhabitable.

In this District the Natives if they wish to burn any swamp or piece of country in the Vicinity of dwellings always come first to ask my permission.

I remain Sir,
Your obedt. Servant

George Eliot
Resident

Even in those days, the wheels of government turned slowly. The outcome, ten months later, was '*An Ordinance to diminish the Dangers resulting from Bush Fires*', passed by the Legislative Council on the 2nd September 1847, on the authority of Frederick Chidley Irwin, the then Governor and Commander-in-Chief.

The advice of those with some understanding of the social and ecological importance of bushfire to the *Noongars* was ignored, in favour of the interests of farming settlers. No doubt this was also to the political liking of the governor, who needed to be seen as someone who took strong action on behalf of the settlers. The Ordinance imposed flogging and imprisonment on Rottnest Island for *Noongars* setting fire to the bush.

-oOo-

Essay 7

Balga, Boodja & Measles

> *'From winter, plague and pestilence, good lord, deliver us…'*
> Thomas Nashe 1567-1601

There is ample documentary evidence that a severe measles epidemic hit south-west Australia in the winters of 1860 and 1861, and another in the winters of 1883 and 1884. The latter epidemic extended to the north-west of the state. These two epidemics, together with diphtheria, whooping cough, influenza, alcohol, venereal disease, and violence greatly reduced the *Noongar* people of the south-west corner, and led most of the survivors to abandon their traditional lifestyle. These survivors left their home country (*boodja*) and moved to the outskirts of settler towns. This reduction in *Noongar* population, and the change in lifestyle of the survivors, must have affected traditional use of fire.

Rottnest Island was used as a prison for *Noongars* from the 1830s to the 1930s. One of the offences punished by sending to Rottnest was firing the bush. Committals of people from the south-west declined sharply after the 1860s. Committals from the north-west declined after the 1880s.

The First Fleet of British ships to arrive in Australia in 1788 took more than 300 days to make the voyage. By the 1850s clipper ships such as the *James Baines* and *Marco Polo* were doing the journey in 60 days, and the introduction of steam ships at about the same time led to further reductions in the voyage time.

In the early years of European settlement, Australia was free of measles, due to the quarantine provided by the long voyage from England. At Fremantle in 1843, Surgeon Dinely wrote *'Measles, small pox, typhus, or puerperal fevers, or any of those dire diseases to which the Mother Country is subject are here unknown.'*

Those passengers who were carrying the virus when they embarked, had either died or recovered by the time they reached Australia. Faster ships, however, enabled the virus to break through. By 1850 measles outbreaks had occurred in Victoria and New South Wales. Tasmania followed in 1854, Queensland in 1857, South Australia in 1859 and Western Australia in 1860.

Measles first arrived in Western Australia in the 1850s, but was successfully quarantined at Fremantle. In 1860, however, the virus arrived in the port of Albany, and spread among the local population, including the *Noongar* people. It then spread up the Albany Highway towards Perth, visiting towns such as Mount Barker, Kojonup, Williams, Beverley, and York.

By 1870 the *Noongar* population had declined noticeably, due to measles, other diseases, and violence. As a result of decreased hunting pressure, the kangaroo population apparently increased. In response to this, the Colonial Secretary, the Honorable F. Barlee, introduced a bill in parliament to repeal the need for a licence to shoot kangaroos.

In the first reading, he was reported in Hansard as saying that *'Kangaroos and other wild animals had increased so greatly, that their destruction was absolutely necessary. The natives were not numerous enough to consume them, and besides they now lived more on flour etc. which they procured from the European population, than on the kangaroo and other animals.'*

Mr. Monger and Mr. Shenton disagreed with the bill on the matter of the *Noongar* need for kangaroo meat. Mr. Monger said that *'The natives to the eastward of York live upon kangaroo, and it would be a great hardship to them if a license was given to have them destroyed'*. Mr. Shenton said that *'Between Perth and Toodyay a number of natives live on kangaroo.'*

Mr. Barlee replied that *'The kangaroos had increased so much while the natives had so decreased that their* [kangaroos] *destruction was necessary as they ate up the natural grasses from sheep and cattle.'* However, Barlee agreed not to pass the bill if it would *'injure the natives'*.

A second measles epidemic broke out in 1883. Governor Broome wrote to the Secretary of State in London:

'I regret to inform you that the disease of Measles has for some time prevailed in this Colony... The last occasion on which Measles was prevalent here was in the year 1861, when it caused great havoc among the Aboriginal population, and also severely affected the Europeans... Some, though not very many, of the Aboriginal natives, have succumbed to the disease at Esperance Bay, in the neighborhood of Albany, and elsewhere... But the native population have not yet been seriously affected as a whole, and certainly it has caused no devastation among them comparable to that which took place when it was epidemic twenty-two years ago. It must be recollected, it is true, that the natives are now much fewer in number; but there are still many in the more Northern Districts, and it is here that I fear grave results.'

Broome's opinion on the relative mildness of the 1883/4 epidemic in the south-west does not match with other reports. In 1933, one European observer, J. E. Hammond, wrote that:

'The measles epidemic of the early 'eighties affected the natives of the South-West and East very much. They died off in great numbers; and the nature of those that were left was altered; they lost all interest in bush life; they did not care what the others did or where they went and they were never the same people again. They dropped their own tongue and used the white man's language; they drifted away from all laws, ceremonies and customs. When their old chief Winjan died in 1884, it was the end of the real Aboriginal of the South-West.' Of course, present day Noongar descendants may not agree with the last comment.

In 1883 the Colonial Surgeon Waylen reported that '...the general death rate was higher than it has been for some years... One or two circumstances have led to this result, chief amongst which may be mentioned an epidemic of measles which, up to the close of the year, had invaded all the Districts of the Colony, and was then spreading. It is 22 years since the last visitation of this malady, so that what in most parts of the world is looked upon as one of the diseases of childhood, became in this Colony one of adult life, frequently assuming a very severe form, characterised by intense fever, delirium, and bronchial complications.'

There is a link between measles virulence and conditions of poor nutrition, overcrowding, and intensive exposure. These are exactly the conditions which Noongars would have experienced at that time, as they were driven off their own country, and forced to share, or compete, with other groups.

In his next report (1884), Colonial Surgeon Waylen noted that 'By the end of the year measles had visited every district, with more or less severity, and but few families escaped; it spread amongst the aboriginals, especially about the Murchison and the Gascoyne, where, owing to exposure and want of proper care and nourishment, many died.'

Dr. Waylen did note that the epidemic was less severe in the south-west than the previous one of 1860/61. There were further outbreaks of measles in 1893, 1898, 1908, 1911, 1915, 1921 and 1924.

In the same year as Governor Broome's letter to the Colonial Secretary, a report on the treatment of Aboriginal prisoners stated that:

'It is a melancholy fact that throughout Australia the Aboriginal Race is fast disappearing... In what may be termed the Home District of this Colony, which is bounded on the North by the Murchison River, on the East by a line parallel to the coast and from 60 to 100 miles from it, and on the South and West by the sea, a great part of which has been occupied nearly fifty years, the fact that the aborigines are fast disappearing is apparent on all sides; and it is a mournful truth that, whatever is done, it appears to be an impossibility to avert this downward course.'

Although the measles epidemics killed many *Noongar* people directly, comments by several Europeans, including Hammond and Daisy Bates in the 1930s, suggest that there was an ensuing effect of deep despair and depression on the survivors. Such despair would lead to self-destructive behaviour such as alcoholism, collapse of family structure, lethal brawling, and a decline in libido and reproduction. Thus the *Noongar* population probably continued to decline for several decades after the epidemics, as older people died and there were few young ones to take their place.

To desert their *boodja*, or traditional country, was the ultimate disaster, because it included their dreaming, connected with the frequently walked footpaths known to *Noongar* people as *bidi-bidi*, and some Europeans as '*songlines*'. These were deeply embedded in creation stories. One probable cause of the desertion was the unavailability of various traditional foods connected with those who had died. Such totemic plants or animals could not be eaten for some time after the death, and with many deaths, so many foods became unavailable that their *boodja* could no longer support the survivors.

By the turn of the century, Daisy Bates found few *Noongars* left in the Swan Valley, or elsewhere in the south-west. She learnt the phrase '*Jangga meenya bomunggur*', which she interpreted as '*the smell of the white man is killing us*'. The sharp decline of indigenous populations from diseases introduced by European colonists was not confined to Western Australia. In New South Wales, N. Butlin has recently written that '… *half the Aborigines between the Hawkesbury and Botany Bay died from smallpox during April and May 1789…*'.

There were also lethal epidemics in North and South America, New Zealand, and Pacific Islands such as Fiji, Tahiti, Samoa and the Cook Islands. Where the inhabitants used fire this affected vegetation. I thank an American writer, Stephen Budiansky, for permission to give a quote from William Wood, a European settler in Massachusetts in 1639, '… *in some places where the Indians dyed of the Plague some fourteene yeares agoe, is much underwood, as in the mid way betwixt Wessaguscus and Plimouth, because it hath not been burned.*' We may wonder if, in this case, '*plague*' means measles, since bubonic plague would have doubtless also affected the Europeans.

There is a strong case for considering disease, and the ensuing depression and self destruction, to be the major cause of decline in indigenous people following colonisation, far exceeding direct violence by firearms.

Report by the Colonial Surgeon on the Public Health of the Colony for the year 1883. Government Printer, Perth.

'...the general death rate was higher than it has been for some years, while the rate of infant mortality was greater, by 2 per cent, than in 1882.

One or two circumstances have led to this result, chief amongst which may be mentioned an epidemic of measles which, up to the close of the year, had invaded all the Districts of the Colony, and was then spreading. It is 22 years since the last visitation of this malady, so that what in most parts of the world is looked upon as one of the diseases of childhood, became in this Colony one of adult life, frequently assuming a very severe form, characterised by intense fever, delirium, and bronchial complications. Measles first made its appearance at Albany, and as it has been suggested that it might have been confined to that locality, I may quote a portion of the report of the District Medical Officer, Dr Rogers, on the subject: 'The first three cases occurred in July, almost simultaneously, and on making inquiries, I found that the three men had all been on board the P&O steamer and down in the fore-hold amongst the Lascar crew, from whom, though not suffering at that time, they, in my opinion, caught the disease...it would, I think, be better that measles should be endemic and a disease of early life, than that it should be epidemic, prostrating whole families at once. Where its ill effects are most noticeable is amongst the aboriginals of the far outlying districts, and those to the eastward of Albany suffered severely. When taken care of, they do well, and this was evidenced in the case of the native prisoners at Rottnest, where out of 120 who took the disease in October and November not one died.'

Report by the Colonial Surgeon (Dr Alfred Waylen, MD) on the Public Health of the Colony for the year 1884, Government Printer, Perth.

'By the end of the year measles had visited every district, with more or less severity, and but few families escaped; it spread amongst the aboriginals, especially about the Murchison and Gascoyne, where, owing to exposure and want of proper care and nourishment, many died; in the Eastern and other more settled districts, where this was afforded them, there were but few fatal cases. As a rule the natives suffered far less than at the former visitation, 23 years since; this may be accounted for from the fact of the malady not spreading until after the end of winter, thus lessening the chance of lung complications.'

Report of the Central Board of Education for the year 1883, Government Printer, Perth.

'Had it not been for a very severe epidemic which made its appearance during the last quarter of the year in the form of measles, which seriously affected the attendance at most of the schools, we should have been able to show a very considerable increase, not only in the number of children on the rolls, but also in the average attendance.'

Report of the Central Board of Education for the year 1884, Government Printer, Perth.

'Although, during the early part of 1884, the attendance was very seriously affected at some of the Schools, especially in the Southern Districts, by the epidemic (measles) which had been raging so severely during the latter portion of 1883...'

-oOo-

Essay 8

Mudballs, Microbes & Memsahibs

'One may not doubt that, somehow, good
Shall come of water and of mud...'
Rupert Brooke, *English Poet 1887-1915*

I have read that in parts of India, when they want to start a new rice field, they traditionally go to an old one, and make balls of mud from the soil therein. These they put in the sun to dry. They then level the new field, build banks around it, flood it, and fling in the mudballs. In former colonial days, this behaviour might well have puzzled onlooking *sahibs* and *memsahibs*, and been scorned as *'unscientific'*, but European science has only recently caught up with the Indian farmers. The mudballs inoculate the new field with *cyanobacteria* from the old, so enabling nitrogen fixation, and a better rice crop.

Similar to rice, cycad plants from around the world depend on nitrogen-fixing *cyanobacteria* (*Nostoc*) in their roots. *Nostoc* flourishes best after fire, in part due to the alkalinity of ash. The West Australian cycad, *djiridji* (*Macrozamia riedlii*), is no exception. In the *jarrah* forest of south-west Australia the benefits of increased availability of nitrogen, and other nutrients, after fire, are obvious for three to four years. This was well described in a fine paper by several local scientists (Grove *et al.* 1980).

Together with lightning, we can regard the long lived *djiridji*, and short lived nitrogen fixing legumes (*Fabaceae*), as the engine room of the *jarrah* forest. The legumes fix nitrogen in root nodules through the bacterium *Rhizobium*. *Coondli* (sheoak or *Allocasuarina* spp.) also fix nitrogen. Since nitrogen is essential to all life, without the nitrogen fixed in the engine room, the *jarrah* forest would collapse, as would most of the wildlife within it. Interestingly, the bacterium *Rhizobium* in legume roots, like *Nostoc* in the

41

cycads, fixes nitrogen vigorously for only three to four years after fire. The legumes then senesce, and await the next fire.

Early Europeans settlers, their present descendants, and current *Noongar* Elders, have described past traditional burning in the south-west corner of Australia. For example, most *jarrah-marri* forest will just carry a mild, patchy fire every two to four years. Such mild fires could be lit, and tended, in bare feet. They could be easily swatted and guided with green branches. They left unburnt patches as refuges. Like the Indian villagers with their mudballs, Aboriginal people knew, and still know, things that some European academics clearly don't.

As discussed previously (Essay 5), there is strong evidence, from fire marks on over five hundred old *balga* grasstree stems, that most of the *jarrah-marri* forest was, at least up to the First World War, burnt patchily every two to four years. This is confirmed by some present day *Noongar* Elders. Such burning would have maintained better nitrogen fixation, and hence better forest health, than current blanket fire intervals of fifteen or twenty years, followed by intense fires. The sickness of *jarrah* trees, and understorey shrubs in long unburnt areas is rather obvious. Leaves are small and discoloured, and wildflowers are few.

Given the tendency for decay to lead to acidification, which inhibits *Nostoc*, does fire exclusion for decades make sense? Some assume that long fire free periods are needed to build up seed banks, but is this assumption true? From my observations, it is simplistic.

Some seeds last a long time, but others actually decline after only a few years, due to ant and weevil predation, and mould attack. Also, due to nutrient lock-up in unburnt dead matter, seeds may look sound on the outside, but turn out to be empty husks. Very fierce fires, after long intervals, must incinerate a large proportion of the seed bank, which is suspended in the leaf litter.

The claim that weeds follow fire is true, but is a misleading half truth. Long unburnt areas can also be severely infested with weeds, including the notorious Bridal Creeper. Under long fire exclusion, some native plants themselves become invasive weeds. Examples are Parrot Bush, Rock Sheoak, and Bull Banksia, which smother other native plants. Bull Banksia is a notorious host for the mould *Phytopthora cinnamomi*, which kills *jarrah*.

Those of us who have worked in the bush have long noticed problems with the health of *marri* trees. They bleed gum, and their bark is rotting. They are immune to the mold *Phytopthora cinnamomi*, so are they starved of nutrients? Are they succumbing to those fungi which thrive in long unburnt areas, or are they perhaps deprived of the *mycorrhizae* which thrive in recently burnt areas? Are those who urge long fire exclusion, based on the rhetorically alliterative Orwellian chant that *'burning destroys biodiversity'*, actually themselves potentially guilty of large scale forest destruction by lack of available nitrogen, not to mention exposing human lives and property to uncontrollable summer fires in heavy fuel?

Other people may have other ideas about the interaction between fire and the nitrogen supply of the *jarrah* forest. Medieval universities engaged in vigorous disputes, based on Plato's dialectic approach of *thesis*, *antithesis* and *synthesis*. More recently, philosophers such as G.W.F. Hegel, have recommended dialectic as a road to truth. Essays such as this can play a part in building roads to truth, without the stilted, sometimes obscure language of a refereed journal, not to mention the occasional obtuse referee.

I am not a member of any political party, but I have met some likeable Greens, and think their party would get more support, especially in country electorates, if they publicly adopted a more rational policy on the constructive use of deliberate burning, in line with traditional burning by *Noongar* people. We newcomers can learn much from their traditions.

-oOo-

Essay 9

History, Humus, and Charcoal

'History is not only a valuable part of knowledge, but opens the door to many parts, and affords materials to most of the sciences.'

David Hume (1711-1776)

Some, but not all, scientists dismiss history as unreliable, irrelevant, or second rate knowledge. Some of the dismissive scientists, in an attempt at glib dismissal, have misused the term 'anecdotal', which means 'not published'. Perhaps they were searching for the word 'apocryphal', meaning 'unreliable'. Historians take a deeper view.

Some people, possibly suffering from physics envy, may hope that ecology is pure science. In fact, it is a mixture of science and humanities, including history, philosophy, anthropology, psychology, botany and zoology, and a few other odds and ends.

As a matter of history, early European settlers in Western Australia came mainly from the British Isles, with a cool, temperate climate. As a matter of culture and psychology, they brought with them ideas about soil, and gardening, which may be true in cool, temperate lands, but are not necessarily true in Australia.

One of these ideas is that humus is essential for healthy plant growth, since it holds nutrients and moisture. That is true if, like me, we all want to grow cool, temperate gardens, with snapdragons and nasturtiums. However, in the West Australian climate, humus is highly fugitive. Most gardeners will have noticed that, if they started the summer with a pot full of soil, rich in humus, by autumn they had less than half a pot left. The humus has, if kept moist, rotted away, fleeing upward as carbon gas, and downward as carbonic acid. If it has been allowed to dry out, it may have blown away, as fertile dust, on the east wind, presumably ending up somewhere in the Indian Ocean. There it possibly benefits the phytoplankton, and so the fish.

44

Ecology is full of such intriguing possibilities, often overlooked by some investigators.

Before European arrival, I'm sure there were some pockets of humus in the *jarrah* forest, for example, amongst rockpiles, or along moist creek banks. Most of the forest, however, carried little humus. Being frequently burnt by *Noongars*, it had plenty of ash. So much that they had precise words for different types of ash. According to Rose Whitehurst's dictionary, they carefully distinguished between black charcoal (*kop*) and white quicklime (*yoort*). These have different effects upon soil.

The tiny tunnels in *kop* provide habitat for beneficial microbes, and *yoort* makes magnesium and calcium available to plants. *Yoort*, when slaked by rain or dew, also raises soil pH, with benefits to the nitrogen fixing activities of *cyanobacteria* such as *Nostoc*.

In 1837, a visitor to Perth, James Backhouse, wrote that '*The streets are of sand, mixed with charcoal, from the repeated burning of the scrub, which formerly covered the ground, on which the town stands...The Natives are now setting fire to the scrub, in various places, to facilitate their hunting, and to afford young herbage to the kangaroos...*'.

The ash provided some of the nutrients, and the charcoal stored these nutrients and moisture, plus some useful soil microbes, as humus does in temperate climates. Smoke germinated plenty of legumes, which fix nitrogen, but they, like *djiridji* (*Macrozamia riedlii*) only do this for three to four years after a fire. Through long fire and smoke exclusion we are starving the *jarrah* forest. We have largely lost the native grasses, which provided grazing for kangaroos, and shelter for smaller creatures.

In 1845 James Drummond, the first government botanist, found some seeds when digging a well near the Swan River. He noted that, '*These seeds or involucres, were dug up when sinking a well on the alluvial banks of the Swan River, they were mixed with charcoal, for charcoal is invariably found in the alluvial deposits of the rivers in this country, to a depth which seems to prove that the present race of natives or others having a similar habit of annually burning the country must have inhabited these districts for a much longer period than can be ascertained by any sort of people, not excepting the Chinese.*'

Earlier, in 1841, the Reverend John Wollaston complained, in his journal, about the charcoal in the sand. He wrote that '*The dust of this country creates the greatest inconvenience and adds greatly to the trouble of washing, together with the sand it contributes to the speedy destruction of shoes and stockings. It is as impalpable as the finest flour. Charcoal enters largely into its consumption from the immense quantity of burnt wood over the face of the land...*'.

Even earlier, in 1829, a Royal Navy surgeon at Albany, Dr. J.B. Wilson, wrote that '*The land we passed over today was for the most part composed of charcoal, and other vegetable matter, varying in depth from four to twelve inches, under which was sand about six inches deep.'*

Ecologists and gardeners can learn from science, but also from history. I love my nasturtiums and roses, but some native plants are adversely affected by moist humus, suffering collar and root rot. Long fire exclusion from the *jarrah* forest in general, is putting native plants, including *jarrah*, in danger. I remember seeing an *'environmentalist'* joyfully spread deep, fertile mulch in the bush, thinking he was helping the plants. In fact in the next winter it promoted the lethal honey fungus, *Armillaria luteobubalina*. Black from fire is not ugly, as some, due to cultural baggage, believe. In my view it goes very nicely with green.

-oOo-

Essay 10

Conflagrations and Crepuscular Critters

> *Wee, sleeket, cow'rin, tim'rous beastie*
> *O, what a panic's in thy breastie!'*
>
> Robert Burns, November 1785

It is over sixty years since I last saw Mr. Donald Stamp, BA. He taught me English, and was one of those lovable teachers who can breathe life into a subject. Think of Robin Williams in the film 'Dead Poets Society' and you get the picture. Donald Stamp introduced us to George Orwell's writing, and showed us how every sentence was clear as a pane of glass. He laughed with us at Mr. Micawber's *'peregrinations'* in the metropolis. He loved *'The Lake Isle of Innisfree'* by William Butler Yeats, and the poetry of Robert Burns.

Imagine Donald's dismay if, instead of the evening being full of the linnet's wings, Yeats had written a scientific paper called *'Auditory and Visual Signals from the Crepuscular Avifauna (Carduelis cannabina) of a Small Hibernian Island'*, or Burns had written about *'The Habitat and Alarm Signals of a Small Murid Rodent (Apodemus sylvaticus)'*. Donald might have told us to rip it out of the book. So, while I find ecology a fascinating and important subject, I do get a little impatient with the obscure and pretentious language used by some ecologists.

I am not the first grumpy old man to do so. In 1973 Sir Ernest Gowers, an eminent authority on clear use of language, translated an impressively opaque paragraph of eco-gobbledygook. It was more than forty words long, and from a refereed journal. He concluded that it meant that animals move about more than plants, and when they have moved, they are no longer in the same place.

I have never seen a Honey Possum, but from photographs, and the academic research, I get the impression of an appealing little creature, coming out at twilight, twitching its nose in search of its supper of pollen

47

or nectar. They would have had to move cautiously, since they would not have been alone. Apart from hungry *Noongars*, they must have offered a juicy morsel for other predators. Perhaps owls, with their adaptations to hunting in twilight, or snakes which can detect warmth.

So it was with mixed feelings that I set out upon a journey into the hinterland of scientific literature on the Honey Possum (*Tarsipes rostratus*), or more properly, the *noolbenger*. In loyalty to Donald Stamp, I have tried to keep my own language plain and simple. If I have failed, I apologise, and will try to do better in future. At my age there may not be many future occasions. Meantime, I am busy planting bean rows, and listening for the linnet's wings.

Academic research into the *noolbenger* probably started in the 1970s, although I am sure the *Noongar* people knew a fair bit about the matter long before that, and some may still. The very name *noolbenger* shows that *Noongar* people were well aware of it, and would have also known something about its relationship with fire. A prominent *Noongar* man, Glenn Kelly, once wrote an interesting article on traditional *Noongar* use of fire near the south coast. Drawing upon his older family members, he mentioned the '*bridya*', an important Elder who had authority to decide on when and where to burn. According to Glenn Kelly, such burning was generally more frequent in the past, and hence milder and patchier, with deliberate protection of some patches for longer periods.

It would be worth asking *Noongar* Elders if they know anything about *noolbengers* and fire. The older women may be more knowledgeable than men about plants and small animals, and could probably best be approached by a female researcher of *Noongar* descent. I strongly suspect that *Noongars* would have eaten the wee beasties.

If *Noongars* did harvest *noolbengers*, they would not necessarily have waited until the local population was at its maximum. It can be shown, by simple mathematics, that a greater total harvest in the long term can be made by regular harvesting before the sigmoid population growth curve peaks. Besides, I doubt if *Noongars* bothered much with sigmoid growth curves, but simply used their eyes and judgement, and perhaps information held as very old songs or stories about the particular walk track they were using.

The first academic publication I can find on *noolbengers* is, surprisingly, from the Missouri Botanical Gardens, USA, in 1979. The present most published West Australian academics seem to be Professor Don Bradshaw, of the University of Western Australia, and Professor Ron Wooller, of Murdoch University, who was involved in the Missouri paper. Their studies have been mainly on diet, metabolism and other physiology, and I expect this is true and useful. They have also made comments on the effect of bushfire on *noolbengers*.

They both suggest that the animal is adversely affected by fire, but, as far as I can see, their studies do not reveal how soon the population recovers after a fire, and whether it is then larger, or smaller than before the fire. Nor do they seem to have studied a wide enough range of different fires to see if decline and recovery may differ for fires of differing intensity and extent. If I am wrong on this point, I will listen courteously to other views.

Scales of space and time are important in bushfire ecology, if only to avoid pointless disputes. Studying fire effects over only a few weeks, months or years, at small scales of tens, or even hundreds of metres, may give answers that conflict with the observations of practical fire managers, dealing with scales of many kilometres, time spans of decades, and a wide range of fuel, weather, and terrain. Both parties may be right, in their own context, as long as they do not dogmatically try to claim universal truth.

Some of Professor Bradshaw's honours students once posted a forty page article on the Worldwide Web, but it may have now been withdrawn. They cited research saying that fire reduces *noolbenger* numbers, but again did not say for how long, or over what area, nor what sort of fire they were talking about, with regard to intensity, rate of spread, area, or patchiness. Land managers, such as DBCA, have to deal with space and time, and fire intensity and rate of spread. Are large fierce fires, after decades of fire exclusion, likely to cause a greater, or longer lasting decline in animal populations, than milder, patchier, more frequent fires? My own observations of intensely burnt sites suggest they are. There are good reasons to expect that recovery time is related to the last fire's intensity and area. Small, frequent, therefore mild and patchy burns surely kill fewer plants and animals, and small areas so burnt recover sooner, than large areas completely blackened by flames from hell, due to inappropriate long fire exclusion.

At their study site, the students were unable to show a statistically significant difference between *noolbenger* numbers in burnt and unburnt areas in summer, but claimed a difference in winter. This was, however, based on a very small sample, and the local flowering of an attractive food plant may have skewed the result. Fire managers, and the rest of us, are left wondering what the truth is. Clearly more research is needed, perhaps designed, analysed, and interpreted by a competent statistician, with due attention to possible false assumptions, and the possible omission of some relevant information.

A National Parks Ranger once told me that *Noolbengers* occur in John Forrest National Park. If this is so, then we should consider the yet unpublished fact that there is strong evidence, from fire marks on old *balga* stems, that the *jarrah* ridges in John Forrest NP were burnt, before European settlement, every 3-4 years; the midslopes, with some *marri* litter, every 2-3 years, and the grassy, clay *wandoo* flats every second year. If *noolbengers* were there, how did they survive? People with practical fire experience will appreciate that consistent burning at those frequencies will automatically leave unburnt patches, including the occasional unburnt grasstree thatch. Current fire intervals of decades lead to very fierce fires, leaving few, if any unburnt patches or grasstrees.

The literature reports that male *noolbengers* have a home range of thousands of square metres, females rather less. During the day, *noolbengers* very sensibly hide in thicker patches of bush, presumably as close as possible to food, with an eye to a possible romantic encounter.

Although it has a different diet, we may compare the case of the New Holland Mouse (*Pseudomys novaehollandiae*). This small animal has attracted more research than the *noolbenger,* and the conclusion from two published studies is that it does best in recently burnt, regrowing bush, reaching maximum abundance 2-3 years after fire. This may be due to the floral richness peaking at that time. A mosaic of different aged patches is generally recommended in research into these animals. Mention is made of their incineration, and local extinction, by fierce fires. As an attempt at instant dismissal, some will say that you can't compare a mouse in Victoria with a *noolbenger* in Western Australia. I think, in fact, such comparison is valid and useful.

If, in *noolbenger* country, fire is artificially withheld for decades, we know that dead matter will, undeniably, build up. In hot, dry, windy weather a fire can then be fierce, all consuming, and unstoppable, at least by human means. Both food and shelter in an area of thousands of square kilometres may be completely burnt out by a single fire. In the hottest places, the soil seedbank will be largely incinerated. Few, if any, *noolbengers* will survive in that large area, and it will take a long time for them to recolonise it, given their small size, and the lack of unburnt refuges. The open nature of the burnt area will expose any survivors to predators.

It is most unlikely that such a situation could have existed before European arrival, even if there had been no *Noongars* with their firesticks. Lightning fires alone would have formed a coarse, stable, self-organising mosaic. *Noongar* burning would have added areas of finer grained mosaic. These facts have inevitable implications for future *noolbenger* fire management in Australia.

Noolbengers play an important, even if not exclusive, role in the pollination of some plants. If plants germinate, resprout, and flower in a large burnt area, with no pollination, or reduced pollination, they may not start to build up a viable seed bank until the *noolbengers* return. Studies of the recovery time within large burnt areas, where *noolbengers* are like tiny fish breeding up in a vast ocean, may be misleading. Smaller, or more patchily burnt areas probably recover much faster. This multi-scale research needs to be addressed. Until it is, we have no clear scientific guidance on the best way to manage fire in *noolbenger* habitat.

Common sense suggests that a fine grained mosaic (patches of tens to hundreds of square metres) of burnt and unburnt will be best, offering both food and shelter within a short distance. This will also protect the *noolbengers* from the all-consuming effects of large (thousands of square kilometres) bushfires, some with the characteristics of firestorms.

-oOo-

Essay 11

Truth, Glory and Gravy

'Beware of false prophets, which come to you in sheep's clothing,
but inwardly they are ravening wolves.'

St Matthew, ch.7, v. 15

There have been so many Australian bushfire enquiries over the last few decades, that it would be tedious to repeat the truths that have been previously submitted by so many people experienced in the matter, and even more tedious to repeat the nonsense submitted by those inexperienced in bushfire, but thirsting to expound their theories in a public arena. Such theories may be based on copious publication lists, rather than on practical experience.

A French philosopher, Simone Weil, once suggested that one view of science is that of a game of chess, with competitions, prizes, and medals. On another occasion, she suggested that *'Culture is an instrument wielded by professors to manufacture professors, who in turn manufacture more professors'*. This is extreme, as there are many fine professors. Yet there are other professors who use their title to publicly push a particular political and ideological point of view, mixing science with rhetoric.

Since its origin, ecology has grown into a much inflated game of chess, associated with those other roads to glory and medals, environmentalism and politics. If it is a science, then ecology should aim for the truth, but there are, sadly, problems with human vanity, greed, cunning, and jealousy. From time to time, some ecologists have published false information, or omitted information. Some have also aggressively tried to ridicule anything which does not conform to their opinions.

They may be unaware that Francis Bacon spotted this human tendency in 1625, when he wrote that those who do not understand something, will immediately ridicule it, so hoping to make their foolishness seem like wisdom. Bacon was not the first to note such behaviour.

Nearly a thousand years ago, the Persian poet, philosopher, and mathematician, Omar Khayyam, wrote bitterly that some of his contemporaries tried to *'mingle truth with falsehood'*. He described how they would ridicule honest scholars. It is a comforting thought that today we remember Omar rather than his critics.

In recent times some more truthful people have become uneasy at the direction academic bushfire ecology is taking. In Australia it has been carried along by tax payer funded gravy trains. Some refereed journals of ecology have become oddly selective in what they publish.

To dispel the bad smells of some academic ecology, let's open the window to the fresh breeze of geometry. Triangles are intriguing shapes, for example six equilateral triangles form a hexagon, and hexagons tessellate beautifully to infinity. Equilateral triangles form the basis of the Platonic solids, with wonderful Greek names, such as dodecahedron, or icosahedron. Unsurprisingly, humans have found many uses for triangles, such as rigid structures in building and engineering.

Honest academics have devised useful trinitarian models, such as Albert Atterberg's sand-silt-clay triangle, and Kenneth Boulding's economic triangle, of robbery-exchange-giving. Poor old Kenneth was shunned by some of his profession, apparently for being too lucid.

I believe an English biologist once made an interesting triangular model of bird behaviour in nesting colonies. He defined three behaviour types, called *suckers, cheats*, and *grudgers*, based on their attitude to requests from other birds for mutual grooming of the inaccessible back of their heads. *Suckers* always complied, but gave more grooming than they received. *Cheats* received grooming, but then failed to respond. *Grudgers* only groomed *cheats* once. Interestingly, the *grudgers* became most abundant in the long run.

Might triangles be useful in understanding the situation in current bushfire ecology? The illustration shows a triangle in which ecologists can be plotted. Those solely motivated by the truth will appear at the top vertex. Those who see bushfire ecology mainly as a road to glory will appear at bottom right. Those seeking a ride on the gravy train of grants, fame, and travel to conferences in exotic places will appear at bottom left. Being mere humans, most ecologists, including me, will have mixed motives, but will appear somewhere inside the triangle.

The triangle can be divided into three zones, which we can label A, B and C grade ecologists. Most ecologists will have little difficulty in placing other ecologists in one of these zones, but we may have more difficulty in placing ourselves.

```
                    100% ▲ 0%

    TRUTH      50%   ╱ A ╲   50%    GLORY
                  ╱  C │ B  ╲
          0%    ╱─────┴─────╲    100%
            100%      50%      0%

                    GRAVY
```

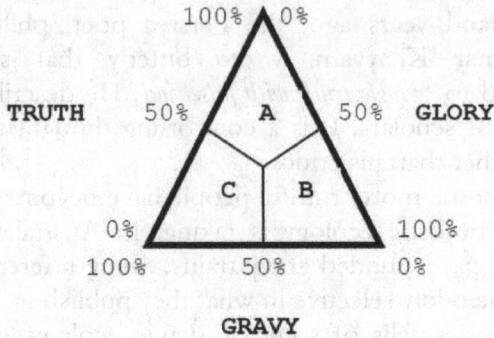

There is a parallel example from the humanities. In his interesting book '2½ Pillars of Wisdom', Professor Alexander McCall Smith has delicately sketched the case of Professor Doctor Moritz-Maria von Igelveld, an expert on Portuguese irregular verbs, who spends a large part of his life travelling to far off conferences. At these, he bores the audience close to death. He then returns to his university, looking very serious and important, and writes further boring papers. His loyal secretary is always greatly impressed by the papers she types up after these events. I am sure she also types the press releases.

There are similar experts in Australia, connected with ecology, bushfire, biodiversity, and impending catastrophic climate change. I have met a few, and hope I never meet any more. When they appear on television, I quickly turn it off.

As an afterthought, the truth-glory-gravy triangle might also be a useful framework for assessing politicians, especially at election time. After all, they are the ones who largely decide how much tax payers' money is devoted to ecological research, and which ecologists they will believe and support. We voters should clearly give our support to those politicians and ecologists who are well inside the truth zone.

Calling once more on Francis Bacon, we may remember his words, '*Nothing doth more hurt in a state than that cunning men pass for wise*'. Francis was, of course, politically incorrect. He overlooked the existence of cunning women. I must emphasize that there are many politicians and ecologists, of either gender, who actually seek and tell the truth. Long may they live.

-oOo-

Essay 12

Good Thinkers, Grass, & Bushfire in Denmark

'One good thinker is worth two good workers'.
The English grandmother of A.B. Adams

Readers unfamiliar with the beautiful southern coast of Western Australia may find their minds skipping to wonderful Copenhagen, but the Denmark discussed here is a small town on that beautiful southern coast, named after a Dr Alexander Denmark, by one of his colleagues, Dr Wilson of the Royal Navy. Wilson explored the area in 1829, soon after the foundation of a British garrison at King George's Sound, now known as Albany. The garrison was intended to keep the French out of the area, but the two squabbling nations were amazingly bad mannered, to say the least, in overlooking the fact that the country already belonged to the indigenous *Noongar* people, who had been there for tens of thousands of years. That far back, my ancestors, and those of all Royal Navy officers, were probably living in caves, perhaps dining on woolly mammoth steaks.

In 1907 a young Englishman called A.B. Adams settled at Denmark. He had an agricultural background, and took up farming. There are still areas of giant *karri* tree at Denmark, but at that time settlers concentrated on clearing the rather smaller *jarrah* and *marri* trees. Even this was heavy work. Forty years later, Arnold Adams wrote an article on his experiences, which was published in the Western Mail newspaper (9th January 1947).

In it he made some interesting observations on the *jarrah-marri* forest near Denmark, which are relevant to the past and present bushfire situation in the area. He was not only a good worker, but also a good thinker.

He mentioned Kangaroo Grass (*Themeda triandra*) as the chief grazing growing on the better soils, together with Wallaby Grass (*Danthonia*) and a ground creeper, the red flowered runner (*Kennedya*). Apparently Kangaroo Grass soon disappeared after grazing by farm animals started, except on the best soils (described by Arnold as derived from *epidiorite*), or where fenced against stock.

Some settlers, with sheep, might have been glad to see it go, since its spiky seed heads get tangled in fleece. The initial widespread presence of this grass is clear evidence that the area had been subject to former widespread and frequent burning, which is essential for the long term survival of Kangaroo Grass. Although lightning can cause occasional, irregularly timed fires, deliberate burning by *Noongar* people, perhaps over tens of thousands of years, was the only possible cause of fire frequent and regular enough to maintain this grass.

Research in both South Africa and Australia shows that to flourish, Kangaroo Grass needs burning in dry conditions, every 2-4 years. Otherwise it eventually smothers under its own thatch, and gradually disappears from the site. There is a considerable literature on this grass, which occurs in many places in the south-west Pacific region, around the Indian Ocean, and in east, west, and southern Africa. It is maintained by human use of fire, and some useful botanical thinkers have ventured into human ecology, and suggested that its wide distribution is due to the interactions between frequent fire, grass, grazing animals, and migrating humans.

In southern Africa burning was maintained by *Bantu* graziers, to generate feed for their goats and cattle, and to reduce ticks. They probably learned the importance of frequent grass burning either from the previous inhabitants, the hunter gatherer *Xhoisan* people; or from their own ancestral origin in West Africa, more than a thousand years ago.

Grass fires are still common in the drier parts of West Africa, because people still burn the grass for the above mentioned reasons of grazing and tick reduction. As one example, *Themeda* occurs in Senegal, and a recent group of three researchers found that traditional burning by African graziers there showed a '*high degree of awareness about the application of fire*', and that this should be recognised in government policy decisions (Mbow *et al.* 2000)

In the already mentioned observation by Captain Henry Stokes R.N., he remarked on the animated fun *Noongar* people got out of burning, and their mastery of carefully controlled fire, beating it out with green branches. European foresters used the same technique to control fires up to the nineteen twenties, but after that fires became too fierce. Anyone trying to control a fire with green branches today would probably be removed from the fire ground as a dangerous lunatic.

To *Noongar* people, Kangaroo Grass would have been especially entertaining to burn, as it makes a lively crackling and popping noise, and does not give as much fierce radiant heat as the current turpene soaked bark, seed capsules and leaf litter in *jarrah-marri* forest litter, which build up to dangerous levels when fire is excluded for more than four years. Avoiding radiant heat would have been important to *Noongars*, since they burnt in summer, in bare feet, and sensibly wore few if any clothes. Besides, when the grass grew again, as the name suggests, it was attractive grazing for kangaroos, an important food for *Noongars*. I'm sure they knew, and may still know, as much about the ecological aspects of fire and Kangaroo Grass as all the academics in Australia and South Africa put together. This is a good example of Plato's *gnosis*, or knowing by experience. I wish I knew the *Noongar* name for Kangaroo Grass, so I could habitually use it.

South African historians have mentioned that what is there called *Rooi Gras* (Red Grass) was the main grazing for the cattle of *Africaner Voortrekkers*, escaping, in the 1830s, from the imposition of British rule at the Cape of Good Hope. Its prolific growth was due to burning by the resident *Bantu* graziers, every few years, in the dry season. Before coming to Western Australia, Mr Adams had spent a few years farming in South Africa, and was perhaps familiar with the grass's history and fire ecology in that country.

Mr Adams also made some comments on forest clearing methods by Europeans at Denmark in the opening years of the twentieth century. He described the better country as red gum forest (we may assume *marri*, or *Corymbia calophylla*), which could be cleared by ring barking the trees, and burning them. Once ring barked, such country carried good grass, and would carry a fire *'every year if this was thought desirable'*. The research mentioned above, both in Australia and South Africa, suggests Kangaroo Grass will only carry fire at a minimum of two years, when the seed heads have formed. Perhaps after forty years Mr. Adams had confused annual with biennial burning, or was talking of other grasses in the area.

However, it is worth considering that there is a very similar grass, known as *Themeda quadrivalvis*, which has an annual life cycle. Recent genetic research suggests that, apart from its annual habit, it is difficult to distinguish from Kangaroo Grass. Although supposedly a native of Nepal and India, it has been found in Queensland, where it is known as Grader Grass, and in the north of Western Australia. Was it, at one time, present in the south of Western Australia? An archaeological pollen survey might be informative.

Mr Adams described *'poorer'* soil (sand and laterite?) as forested with a mixture of *jarrah* (*Eucalyptus marginata*) and *'scattered red gum'* and this soil was not successfully cleared of forest by ringbarking and burning. He said that the burning caused forest to spring up again from seedlings and *'suckers'*, presumably *epicormic* shoots.

Much earlier, on his summer 1830 journey through the eastern *jarrah* forest from Perth to the south coast, Captain Thomas Bannister made a number of comments on the common presence of dark brown loam carrying Kangaroo Grass, which he regarded as a sign of good farming country. He travelled through the district now known as Williams. The Colonial Surveyor, John Septimus Roe, also travelled that route in 1835, and wrote of '*excellent soil*' on the right bank of the Williams River, carrying '*luxuriant grass*'.

Again, a medical practitioner, Dr Joseph Harris, travelled approximately the same route in summer 1835, and mentioned tethering horses in grass '*up to their middle*'. He wrote that '*the country was burned in places, but there were extensive ranges of good land, with plenty of grass, even to the top of the hills*'. The current loss of areas of native grasses is probably mainly due to inappropriately long intervals between fires, and heavy grazing by farm stock, but another cause of heavy grazing was the arrival of rabbits in south-west Australia, about the time of the First World War. Rabbits will extirpate grass, by eating the roots in summer to access moisture. Fire marks on *balga* often show an obvious decline in fire frequency at the time of the First World War.

I am grateful to the Trove website for this seminal information on life at Denmark in the early twentieth century, and I will search for more. I don't think a hard working farmer like Mr A.B. Adams was given to fantasy. I am more convinced than ever that history is a useful cross check on scientific investigations. It can check the most ambitious theories for falsehoods, sometimes in an embarrassing way. Nearly three hundred years ago, an English noble, the Earl of Bolingbroke, remarked that historical letters can '*make truth serve as a stalking horse to error*'.

Even further in the past, Socrates noted that the truth can make some people angry. Natural science papers may follow a line of statistical logic, impressive to the naïve reader, or even journal referee. If, however, they start from false assumptions, such papers may arrive at ludicrous conclusions, such as the idea that fire should be excluded for decades from the forests of south-west Australia, and that such long exclusion would, somehow, benefit those forests. The broader historical evidence, of which only a small fraction appears above, is that it is more likely to destroy them, and that having to fight increasingly fierce bushfires is a sure path to social and fiscal ruin in Western Australia, and other places.

-oOo-

Essay 13

The Other Side of the Hill

'All the business of war, and indeed all the business of life, is to endeavour to find out what you don't know by what you do; that's what I called 'guessing what was at the other side of the hill'.'

The Duke of Wellington, 1885

Even if known by different names, bushfire is not confined to Australia. Africa and Madagascar have long records of deliberate burning by humans, for a range of very practical reasons. In India and Burma, there was a long struggle between European foresters, and villagers who burnt the jungle. There is a vast literature on burning by the original inhabitants of North America. Even France has old records of deliberate burning of forests, shrublands, and bramble patches, for purposes such as clearing, grazing animals, and growing crops.

In this essay, I will not try to cover fire everywhere, because much of that has already been ably done by others. Information in this essay will focus on a few places, which seem to have particular relevance to bushfire in Australia.

Information in this essay will help the reader to determine if my ideas on bushfire in Australia are anomalous on the world scene, or are part of a much larger geographical, historical, and even political picture. I am looking for the lawyer's corroboration, or what the scientist and philosopher William Whewell, in about 1840, dubbed *'consilience'*.

Although some may scorn metaphors as *'unscientific'*, they might follow the Iron Duke's metaphor above. Australian ecologists could learn much about fire by studying bushfire on the other side of the Indian Ocean, where Southern Africa has similar climate, soils and vegetation, and some astute ecologists. It also has a similar human history, with indigenous (*Khoikhoi, Khoisan* and *!Kung*) people burning for thousands of years before being

59

replaced by *Bantu* migrants moving south, and, a little later, by European migrants moving north from the Cape of Good Hope.

After reading about Africa, Australian students of fire can read on to other lands where fire has long played a part in human affairs.

Fire in Africa

In the nineteen seventies, J. Parkington studied the reports of early European travellers in South Africa, and found a description of the *Soaqua* people of the Olifant's River Valley, during the seventeenth century. In the dry summers, they congregated around the lower reaches of the river, for access to fresh water, but in winter, with rainfall, they spread out inland, and gathered plant food. Parkington said that *'Taking advantage of the dry condition of the veld and anticipating the plant growth of the wet season, the Soaqua burned the grass along the banks of the river in the late summer of 1661, and presumably in other years too.'* This sounds like early descriptions of *Noongar* burning and seasonal movement along rivers in south-western Australia.

Again in the nineteen seventies, in an excellent article on south and central Africa, Oliver West, former Chief of Botany and Ecology in then Rhodesia (now Zimbabwe), gives references to observations on fire and humans by early European explorers and hunters, and fire's role in stimulating grass growth, at the expense of woody shrubs and trees. He found that excluding fire and grazing led to loss of grass, and encroachment by shrubs and trees. Long standing human use of fire seems to have been a major factor in maintaining large areas of grassy savannah in Africa.

Oliver West quoted a personal communication from a colleague who described traditional burning by the *Ndebele* tribe, around their capital, Bulawayo. The surrounding grassy savanna was divided into three sectors, and one sector was burnt each year, so giving a three year cycle. This was done to stimulate fresh grass for the cattle, by removing tree litter, for the *Ndebele* believe that tree leaves poison grass. Only in the past few decades has the reality of toxic warfare between plants (allelopathy) been demonstrated in other parts of the world.

Further south, describing an African journey in 1811, the hunter W.F. Burchell noted that Bushmen (*!Kung* people) burnt old grass in order to attract game to the fresh green shoots. He described such regrowth as like a *'field of wheat'*. Where there had been no burning, the green growth was smothered by old grass.

Referring to Bushman use of fire in the early twentieth century, Schapera observed that, in the Okavango area (now part of Botswana), the grassy *veld* was normally burnt at the end of the dry season, in order to promote the growth of roots and bulbs in the coming rainy season. The Bushmen also used fire for hunting, the men spreading around the fire in a semi-circle and driving the game towards other hunters lying in wait.

In south-western Australia, *Noongar* people also used this hunting method. It was described in the eighteen forties, by a missionary priest, Dom Rosendo Salvado. In Africa, Schapera noted that the new grass springing up soon after a fire attracted game into the area. In that land there is a well-known sequence of grazing, with zebra and wildebeest coming in first, followed later by antelope. Australian Aboriginal hunters were, and still are, well aware of the attractions of fresh grass to kangaroos.

Even more recently than Schapera, Marshall, working in Africa amongst Bushmen, said that *veld* fires were common, and were caused by Bushmen, trying to attract game to the post-fire green shoots. He also described how fires ran '*raging before the winds*', until a wind shift blew them back on themselves. He reported being surrounded by as many as '*eight fires at a time*'.

In south-western Australia, the technique of using predictable wind changes (for example the daily summer change from land to sea breeze) to make a fire burn back on itself was still known, in the first half of the twentieth century, to *Yamatji* people in *kwongan* heath land near Geraldton (personal communications from Stan Gratte of Dongara). It was also well-known to some European grazier families with coastal leases between Bunbury and Fremantle (personal communication from Elaine Marchetti of Waroona). Up to the early 1960s, they would light a fire at ten in the morning, in March, on a south-easterly wind, then leave it to its own devices, knowing it would safely self-extinguish when the wind backed around to a south-westerly sea-breeze in the afternoon. In current heavy fuels, such a procedure could be disastrous.

The African term *Bantu* simply means '*people*', and is used by the cattle and goat grazing people of southern and central Africa to describe themselves, much as the original inhabitants of south-west Australia describe themselves as *Noongar*. The *Bantu* graziers, who replaced the Bushmen over most of southern Africa, still use fire for hunting, to harvest honey, to stimulate grass for their cattle, and to get rid of ticks, which climb up tall grass stems to drop onto passing beasts and humans. By use of fire these graziers maintain a grassy savannah, or savannah woodland, where otherwise would be dense thorn scrub.

Marwick (1940) noted that the *Swazi* people (who are *Bantu*) have a detailed vocabulary to describe different stages of grass growth in relation to fire. Recently burnt grass is known as *mshakwindla*, and areas conserved from burning for feeding cattle while the new grass grows are called *sikotsa sokuhlala ubusika*. The general name for unburnt ground is *umlale*, and for recently burnt areas *lilunga*. This special vocabulary suggests that landscape fire has long been important in *Swazi* culture.

Rosemary Whitehurst, in her valuable *Noongar* dictionary, tells us that the *Noongar* people of south-western Australia call unburnt country *bokyt*; unburnt country which needs to be burnt *narrik*; and recently burnt country *nappal*, or *yanbart*. There are special words for the different types of grass which sprang up after fire, such as *kundyl, booboo*, and *boongoort*. *Noongars* distinguish between *yoort* (white ash) and *kop* (charcoal), and use the term *nuariny maalak* for a special fire technique, possibly of burning thickets. I doubt if the *Noongar* language would contain such detailed terms if landscape fire, and its effects, were of little practical interest to *Noongar* people.

In Africa, there has been work on the deliberate use of bushfire in Kruger National Park. Evidence for patch burning in East African savanna has been examined, and the issue of deliberate burning for fuel reduction is very much alive in that part of the world.

Kruger National Park is of particular interest. It is South Africa's oldest game reserve, and in 2001 a fierce bushfire swept through it. Large animals, such as elephant, rhinoceros, and warthog were killed, but the fire also killed twenty-three humans. Of these most were women, gathering thatch grass. We need to understand the historical causes of the severity of this fire.

Originally called the Sabi River Reserve, the area of Kruger National Park must have been subject to the frequent landscape fires of grazier *Bantu* herdsmen for centuries, and hunter-gatherer burning long before that. The first warden, appointed in 1940, was Colonel Stevenson-Hamilton, who favoured frequent burning to renew grass. He knew that grazing animals tended to avoid long grass, which can give cover to lion and leopard. He also knew, like the *Bantu* herdsmen, that long grass harbours ticks, which can debilitate both domestic and wild animals.

His views were contradicted, in 1946, by his successor, Colonel J.A.B. Sandenburgh, who opposed deliberate burning. As a result, much of the game moved into neighbouring areas, where villagers still burnt grass regularly. Being outside the legal protection of the park, the animals were slaughtered in large numbers. According to Brynyard, the exclusion of fire from the park led to an encroachment of woody thorn bush, which was still going on at the time he wrote in 1971.

Apart from immediate effects on game, the unburnt grass and thorn bush provided fuel for fierce fires. In the spring of 1954, over five thousand square kilometres burnt, killing many animals. This fire provoked some thought.

Navashni Govender, a former staff member at Kruger National Park, has outlined to me the history of attempts at fire management in Kruger National Park. Following the massive 1954 wildfire, from 1957 to 1980 there was a return to deliberate burning of blocks of about 4000 hectares, in spring, on a three year cycle. From 1981 to 1991 some variation was introduced in fire frequency and season, in the belief that this was more ecologically sound. But in 1993, academic ecologists decided that only lightning fires were '*natural*', and all other fires should be suppressed. Lightning fires were to be allowed to run, even being helped by park rangers over artificial barriers, such as roads. The result was an outbreak of massive fires in 1996, after a late wet season had led to heavy fuel accumulation. Some of these fires were due to lightning, but others were blamed on refugees fleeing from conflict in Mozambique and Zimbabwe. They were possibly trying to clear thick thornbush, to make walking easier. The lethal fire of 2001 has already been mentioned. After that, Kruger National Park adopted a much more flexible fire policy, with greater reliance on the local knowledge of managers, rangers, and local *Bantu* people.

This is very similar to the policy advocated for the forests of south-western Australia by Conservator Stephen Kessell in 1929. Although initially influenced by the anti-burning views of his predecessor, Charles Lane-Poole, he learnt, from practical experience, that burning was essential. He emphasized the importance of local knowledge, and local capacity to decide when to burn, and to act promptly. Kessell was responding to the reality of increasingly fierce fires under attempted fire exclusion in the previous decade. He also clearly acknowledged the role that knowledgeable humans have long played in determining fire frequency, and so in altering the intensity of fires.

Fire in Madagascar

Not far from Africa is Madagascar, which was a French colony from 1895 to 1960. Although Madagascar is not generally well-known, a scholar called Christian Kull has amply addressed the history and political ecology of fire in that island.

Despite a history of traditional burning in France itself, the French colonial forestry officials, and botanists, were mostly opposed to fire, considering it entirely destructive. They had political and economic influence, because of the commercial value of timber. Other French officials, for example agricultural advisers, were more sympathetic to the villagers, understanding the benefits of fire in maintaining grassland for cattle, destroying ticks, and in repelling, or killing locusts. Nevertheless, the use of fire was made a criminal offence.

The Malagasy villagers resented government interference in their traditional use of fire, and resented the comparison of their traditional burning with what they regarded as real crimes, such as theft or murder, so conflict was inevitable. Burning was not only for practical purposes, but played a recreational and cultural role. The conflict over fire continued after independence in 1960, because the new government adopted the *received wisdom* from France, that fire is *mauvais*. Fire lends itself well to clandestine use, so, despite the power of the state, the villagers burnt, and probably still burn, with a great strategic advantage. Sympathetic officials sometimes turned a blind eye.

Christian Kull notes that the *received wisdom* on fire was firstly based on outmoded ideas from the natural science version of ecology, including the *Vegetation Climax Theory* of Clements (1936), and later on the ideas of the *conservation boom* of the 1980s and 1990s, when *biodiversity* became the 'holy grail'. He suggests that the livelihoods and cultural beliefs of people are essential parts of the ecology of an area.

More recent work in ecology suggests that many ecological outcomes are possible from human intervention in the landscape, and that there is no entirely predictable equilibrium state. Both predictable order, and unpredictable chaos, exist within ecosystems, and landscape is a *nature-society hybrid*. Christian Kull argues that landscape is, therefore, subject to human political negotiation. We should not presuppose that a particular outcome, such as tall, closed forest, is *best*, is achievable, and is not negotiable. I suspect that diversity in the landscape offers the best habitat for a diversity of plants and animals.

My own view is that we should, in ecology, always beware of mechanistic science, and be alert to the possibility that our assumptions may be wrong, or insufficient. According to the physicist Pierre Duhem, and the philosopher Willard Quine, extra hypotheses may subtly hide in the background, until recognized and brought into play. Such extra hypotheses may not be scientific, but historical, philosophical, economic, or political. *Scientism* often ignores these rich *Duhemian webs*, so giving an impoverished version of the world and its ecology, including the landscape ecology of fire.

Christian Kull emphasises the extreme complexity of fire, and says that, in order to resolve land use conflicts, we need to consider not only scientific evidence, but also history, power relations, economics, the *ideological baggage of the groups in question*, and how they interact. He might well be talking about the debate over bushfire in Australia.

Du Feu en France

With its generally temperate climate, Europe is not an obviously fire prone region, although there have been severe summer fires in recent times in southern France, Greece, and Sardinia. It has been pointed out, however, that fire has a long history in Europe, as elsewhere, and has played a role in shaping landscape.

The above view is supported by the research of Dr. Helene Ribet into the traditional use of fire in rural France. where some official correspondence from the eighteenth century makes it plain that shepherds in the Pyrenees and the Massif Central traditionally used frequent landscape fire as a way of making country accessible to stock, to promote grass growth, and to enable crops such as rye and oats. Some French experts believe such fire use may date back to the Bronze Age.

I thank Dr. Ribet for some French fire history. For example, in 1731, in a memoir to the *Intendant d'Auvergne*, a public servant wrote *'les bergers font usage de metter le feu aux bruyères et dans le temps où llea sécheresse les rend les plus combustibles... Le prétexte de ces boutefeux est que les bestiaux à laine et à corne y trouvent mieux à paître.'* [Shepherds make a practice of setting fire to the brambles at the time when the dryness makes them most combustible. The pretext for these bonfires is that sheep and cattle find better grazing there.]

In the same year, another correspondent wrote from Aurillac that *'lorsqu'on met le feu aux bruyères, il y vient l'année d'après une herbe tendre, et la bruyère même qui repousse, fait que les bestiaux paissent dans ces lieux la avantageusement pendant deux ou trois ans.'* [When the brambles are burnt, there is lush grass the year after, also the new bramble sprouts, giving the beasts better grazing in those places for two or three years.]

Yet another wrote, in 1731, from Riom, in the Puy de Dome, disputing the views of an official who opposed burning. He said *'l'auteur de ce mémoire se trompe assurément quand il dit qu'il est inutile de brûler les bruyères. Il y a une bonne partie de la province qui n'aurait presque point de récolte si on se départait de cet usage, et après qu'on a semé une première année en seigle et une autre en avoine, la même terre produit pendant plusieurs années un pacage excellent et ce n'est pas qu'après que les bruyères ont surmonté qu'on recommence a brûler et à ouvrir la terre.'* [The author of this memoir is definitely mistaken when he says that it is useless to burn the brambles. Many people in the province have almost no other source of harvest if they abandoned this method, and after they have sown, in the first year, rye, and the next year, oats, the same soil produces for several years an excellent grazing, and it is not until the brambles have overrun it again that they start burning and clearing.]

Like the Malagasy people, those French villagers who have long used

65

fire for constructive purposes, have never accepted its criminalization by the state. According to Dr. Ribet, they are currently resisting recent attempts, by middle class *'conservationists'* from large cities, at politically enforced fire exclusion. Such city people like to walk in the landscape created by the fires of past villagers, but do not want their aesthetic sensitivity offended by any blackened ground. Beauty is, of course, in the eye of the beholder. Australian Aboriginal people describe unburnt bush as *'dirty'*, and recently burnt bush as *'cleaned up'*.

Fire in the Raj

Another rich source of information on fire is to the north of the Indian Ocean, where traditional burning was common in India and Burma before British and German foresters tried to prohibit, and criminalize it, in the nineteenth century, on 'scientific' grounds. This attempt at fire exclusion created ill-will among the villagers, and was, both in India and Burma, a factor in leading to discontent, and the formation of effective grass roots independence movements.

According to Professor Stephen Pyne, of Arizona, the reasons why Indian and Burmese villagers burnt, and may still burn, their forests and jungles were mainly to promote grass for cattle (*coomrie*), and to create clearings for gardens (*toung-ya*). This jarred with the British, and originally German, concepts of *'scientific'* forestry, which aimed to produce the maximum yield of straight saw-logs. Fire made some timber unsuitable for the saw-mill, although some of the shrewder foresters realized that fire was an integral part of the Indian and Burmese forest systems, and probably had been for thousands of years. Some of these foresters expressed doubts about the long term survival of *teak* (*Tectona grandis*), *chil* (*Pinus longifolia*) and *sal* (*Shorea robusta*) forests if fire were excluded. Although fire scars spoiled some logs, they argued that, without fire, there would be, in the long term, no logs at all.

Forester M. J. Slym presented his ideas on the benefits of fire in *teak* forest to a forestry conference in Rangoon in 1875, but he was told by the President that his talk could not appear in the published proceedings. Furthermore, no reason for this could be mentioned. Presumably Slym's views clashed too much with the *'received wisdom'* on fire exclusion. Slym was, soon after, demoted, but it is unclear if this was a direct result of his heresy. Perhaps it was a warning shot across his bows.

One forester, who enthusiastically embraced the official *'scientific'* view of his superiors on fire was David Hutchins (Essay 4), who enjoyed rapid promotion, a knighthood, and subsequently visited Australia to share the benefits of his wisdom on fire with the humble colonials. He was clearly informed of traditional *Noongar* burning, but chose to dismiss it, presumably as *'unscientific'*. Ignoring local Australian knowledge, and the views of some of his fellow foresters in India and Burma, in 1916 he advocated fire exclusion from eucalypt forests.

A decade before Hutchins visited Australia, one brave soul, identified only as 'H. S.', wrote to the Indian Forester in 1896, questioning the merits of fire exclusion from teak forest in Burma. He described how teak seeds needed the removal of leaf litter by fire in order to germinate. He considered that regeneration of teak, over large areas, was impossible without the help of fire.

'H.S.' also described the fires in Burma, where the best *teak* forests were burnt over every year. For those who did not know Burma, he explained that such fires were completely different from the *'huge forest fires of America'*. Burmese fires were confined to the ground, and advanced slowly through a few inches of dry leaves, with flames usually *'not more than a foot high'*, such that a *'pony will step over them'*. He said that these fires could burn for weeks, and *'travel from one end of Burma to the other'*. I wonder who lit them? There are descriptions of fires in south-western Australia, up to the 1920s, which closely resemble this Burmese description, for example by Wallace, a onetime Conservator of Forests. They trickled along all summer, through a few inches of leaf litter, missing patches, and flaring occasionally where a patch of grass or shrub had been missed by previous fires.

In Burma, in the earliest years of the twentieth century, Forester S. Carr seems to have become exasperated at the official doctrine of fire exclusion. He remarked that those most vocal about fire exclusion were those who had least practical experience of the matter. He asked why, if fire exclusion was beneficial, did *teak* grow faster in the parts of the forest that were regularly burnt?

Nevertheless, in 1906 the authoritarian belief in fire exclusion was still dominant in the Indian Forest Service, even though the longstanding traditional use of fire by Indian and Burmese villagers was clearly recognised. Some European foresters simply thought they knew better, and perhaps they did, if maximisation of short term timber harvesting was the sole aim, without regard to long term forest regeneration, or human safety, or the welfare of the local inhabitants. The mental baggage of the senior forest officials needs to be understood.

The Deputy Conservator of Coimbatore, C.E.C. Fischer wrote, in 1906, that:

'From time immemorial the people of India living in and near forests have been in the habit of burning them whenever they wished and moreover have not thought it in any way incumbent on them to prevent burning or refrain from any act which might cause fire, the burning being generally beneficial from their standpoint. Forests are burnt to obtain new grass, to facilitate the collection of fruit, honey, roots etc.; to facilitate shikar [hunting] and even to render passage through the jungle easier and less dangerous...

Fires being almost entirely due to man are preventible ... we must therefore teach them by the force of example as well as by precept assisted by deterrent punishment meted out to detected incendiarists.'

Fischer's views are remarkably similar to those expressed by some European settlers, in an official correspondence on *Noongar* burning in south-western Australia in 1846. While well aware of traditional *Noongar* use of fire, in 1846 they passed a law prescribing flogging and detention for those caught lighting fires (Essay 6). We may also compare this with the criminalization of fire in Madagascar, under French colonial rule, noted by Christian Kull.

Even a decade after Hutchins visited Australia, an observant forester called E. A. Greswell noted, in 1926, that *chil* forests in India needed fire in order to regenerate. He traced the history of burning in these forests back to the time of Aryan invasions 2,000 years ago. From records kept from about 1900, he judged that the traditional fire frequency was about every three to four years. It will be seen, in other essays, that this is an intriguing cross-match with the traditional *Noongar* fire frequency in the *jarrah* forest, and also with the minimum number of colours needed to colour a mosaic map so that no two adjacent patches are the same colour.

From Greswell's article, the life history of *chil* appears to be similar to that of *jarrah*. It has great coppicing powers, and despite being repeatedly cut back by fires, eventually forms a root strong enough to throw up a dynamic shoot which grows very fast, so saving it from the next fire. He also noted that the firing incidence corresponded roughly to the incidence of *chil* seed years, and had an interesting insight into the sometimes blinkered perceptions of Europeans in an alien environment.

Referring to the fire exclusion imposed by the British foresters, and their German advisers, he finished his article by saying that:

'We talk glibly about following nature and forget that the nature we are visualising may be an [sic] European nature inherited from our training and not an Indian nature. We naturally regard fire and grazing as destructive agencies. We, therefore, intuitively

welcome the proof provided by the few cases in which they are so and by inductive reasoning arrive at general conclusions which may be incorrect if not dangerous.'

The Scottish philosopher, David Hume, who warned in 1748 against the perils of induction (reasoning from particular to general), would have agreed with him. Advances in statistics and probability in the twentieth century have made induction a little safer, but deduction (reasoning from general to particular) is still the safest logical path.

Fire in *Phrygana*

There is a dismissive French quip about foreigners who speak French *'comme un mouton Grec'* (like a Greek sheep). Despite linguistic differences, or even rivalries, southern France and Greece have similar vegetation, and have much in common on fire. The Greek word *phrygana* means a low heath, similar to the *garrigue* of southern France, although even drier. Many of our domestic herbs, such as thyme, sage, and rosemary come from this heath. I know, from direct experience in Cyprus, that walking through such plants, on a hot day, creates a wonderful herbal odour. This is due to volatile oils (terpenes) in their leaves. These essential oils are highly flammable, and fires occur easily in summer, when the oils vaporize. In Australia, terpenes occur in many plants, including the genus *Eucalyptus*. Not only do they burn readily, but if long unburnt they can inhibit seed germination in some other plants.

The Roman poet Virgil, in his version of the Greek saga, the Aeneid, described *'scattered fires, set by the shepherds in the woods, when the wind is right'*. Confirming this, a more recent paper on fire in Greece, by Liacos, attributed much burning to shepherds, seeking fresh grazing by burning a mosaic of small patches. The same author attributed the widespread occurrence of the *maquis* and *garrigue* heaths to past burning by humans.

Some automatically regard the past replacement of tall forest by heath as 'bad', but Liacos reported higher nitrogen content in the burnt soils, and better quality forage. The survival of the shepherds probably depended on their burning for forage. Greek farmers also burnt stubble, so supplying ash as a fertiliser for wheat seedlings, and avoiding seedling chlorosis. Stubble burning reduced weeds and insects.

In recent times, Professor Stephen Pyne has given detailed discussion of fire in southern Europe. He suggests that recent fierce fires in Greece, and elsewhere around the Mediterranean, are partly due to a change in land use, from traditional farming, to holiday villas for wealthy city dwellers. The farmers cared for the land more intensively, for example scavenging firewood, and collecting pine needles for animal bedding. The city people who now own properties in the country allow dense vegetation to flourish, and litter to build up, then wonder why it burns, and threatens their houses.

A highly readable essay by Oliver Rackham, on fire around the Mediterranean, suggests a long association between humans, fire, and vegetation there, and supports Stephen Pyne's views on the reason for recent large fires. In this essay, Rackham also touches on fire in Israel.

Fire in Israel

It seems the heath vegetation in Israel (*batha*) has a similar fire history, perhaps even older than that of Greece. This was suggested in 1973 by a distinguished Israeli ecologist, Zev Naveh, who speculated that paleolithic hunter-gatherers, 50,000 years ago, used fire deliberately to drive game and stimulate a richer plant growth.

One effect of fire was to create more edge habitats ('*ecotones*'), favourable to grasses, bulbs, and herbs. Zev Naveh, in true cross-disciplinary style, called upon the Bible and the Talmud for evidence of the common occurrence, and ecology, of fire in the past. According to Zev Naveh there are at least thirty mentions of fire and its effects in the Bible. Fifteen plant species are mentioned, and fire in connection with forest is mentioned six times.

Naveh also recorded the hostile use of fire as a weapon, by Arab herdsmen, probably for over a thousand years, and an awareness of the fertilizing properties of ashes, and the benefits of fire removing thorny bushes for several years. They can tear the udders of goats and cattle.

After a fire, tree seedlings can appear amongst the geophytes, grasses and herbs. They will, if allowed to grow, often shift the *garrigue* type into the taller *maquis* type, shading out the other plants. According to Naveh, this can occur within 3-5 years. Subsequent failure of grass and herb germination, and geophyte flowering, may not be due solely to shading. Naveh suggests a role for the toxic chemicals, contained in shrub and tree litter, which are destroyed by burning. After a few years these chemicals (terpenes) can reappear, and may inhibit germination. We should remember, from Africa, the *Ndebele* belief that leaves from trees are toxic to grass. Allelopathy has been demonstrated in a number of plants, including Californian chaparral.

Fire in California

Much has been said on landscape fire in North America in general, and it is pointless to regurgitate it here. This section concentrates on fire in California, which has similar climate and vegetation to Western Australia.

With their climate, vegetation, and steep slopes, Californians were involved early in fire debates. In 1972, Marvin Dodge, a Californian forest ranger, published, in a prestigious journal, an article on the problem of forest fuel accumulation. He quoted William E. Towell, of the American Forestry Association, who suggested that efficiency in putting fires out might, in fact, prove to be a problem, as unburnt fuels accumulated, and fire hazard increased. From numerous recent reports of Californian fires it seems he was right.

Richard Minnich, using satellite photographs, has contrasted the present fine-grained fire mosaic in Mexican Baja California, with the obviously coarser mosaic north of the border, where US fire fighters have long tried to suppress fires quickly. This has resulted in chaparral fuel accumulation, and some uncontrollable fires when the Santa Ana wind blows.

As in Australia, this view of fire hazard and history is disputed by some. One paper, by Keeley, claims that the difference in fire mosaics is due to differing climate north and south of the US/Mexico border. However, having carefully inspected the satellite image, I am unconvinced by the climatic argument. I doubt if climate respects political borders quite so neatly.

The debate between Minnich and Keeley in California is, nevertheless, an example of the way in which vigorous dialectic (medieval '*disputatio*') can help us reach the truth, sometimes by seeing the '*contingent hypotheses*' of Pierre Duhem. With a colleague Minnich proposed that the vegetation of southern California was, in the past, a fine grained mosaic of different fuel ages and vegetation types. For example, grass would have prevailed where burning by indigenous *Chumash* people was frequent, with patches, or clumps, of shrubs, such as chaparral, elsewhere. There is evidence that California, before the arrival of Spanish Franciscan missionaries in the 1700s, had a large indigenous population, at least hundreds of thousands. This population was greatly reduced by disease and violence, dropping to only 19,000 in 1900.

Minnich has suggested that large fires, such as those of recent times, were rare or non-existent, before 1900, when southern California had a finer grained mosaic of different burn ages. Quoting Stephen Pyne he suggested that over-zealous fire suppression by US authorities, since the 1920s, has

71

led to a coarse mosaic of heavy fuel, and extensive areas of chaparral, which burn uncontrollably when the dry Santa Ana wind blows.

Keeley has taken the contrary view that large fires have always occurred in southern California, and nothing can be done to prevent them. He offered an account of a large fire (~ 125,000 hectares or more) in 1889. Goforth and Minnich contended that newspaper reports of the fire size and ferocity were exaggerated. Relying on such records as property ownership and insurance claims, they estimated that the 1889 fire was much smaller, possibly only a fraction of the size claimed.

Keeley and Zedler gave further evidence to support the claim that the 1889 fire was as big as previously claimed, and offered ingenious arguments against the value of fuel mosaics, involving the use of cellular models of fire spread. They pointed to low lightning frequency in California, and suggested that the present growth in human population has led to more ignitions. However, most of California's current population lives in large coastal cities, and I doubt if many have either the inclination, or the opportunity, to set fires. The Chumash people, living in hutted villages, had both the opportunity and the motive.

In an earlier paper, Keeley acknowledged the likely role of the previous native population in causing ignitions and so changing vegetation, and conceded that a 'substantial fraction of the landscape was converted from shrubs to grass by native American burning.' Yet, in contradiction, he later maintained that there was no fire induced vegetation mosaic in pre-European settlement California.

We could trace this long and involved argument much further, but there is a different, and historically deeper perspective, which may shed light on it. Before Europeans arrived, *Chumash* were present in southern California for at least 13,000 years. Like Australian Aborigines, they were greatly reduced in numbers by disease and violence, firstly from Spanish settlers, then Mexican rulers, then settlers from the United States.

Two scholars, one of them of native American descent, give an Indian population of several hundred thousand in the 1700s, reducing to only 19,000 by 1900. Given that hunter-gatherers, in areas of flammable vegetation, commonly made deliberate use of landscape fire, it is reasonable to conclude that, before European arrival, hundreds of deliberate, or accidental, fires were lit each year.

There are reports of *Chumash* people using landscape fire to promote grassland, including food and medicine plants, and for hunting, in particular of rabbits, which would have been difficult to catch in dense, prickly chaparral. Jan Timbrook, of the Santa Barbara Museum, has given ethnobotanical evidence that landscape fire was used by *Chumash* to

72

promote food and medicine plants. It would be very unusual if the formerly numerous indigenous people of southern California did not use landscape fire as a tool to hunt, and modify vegetation into a mosaic to suit their needs. In fact it would be unbelievable.

Before quitting North America, we should consider the views of an experienced US fire chief on the social aspects of fire. In a talk to the Australian Fire Authorities Council, in Perth, Western Australia, Dr. Jerry Williams, Director of Fire and Aviation Management for the United States Forest Service, set out his thoughts on the fire problem in the USA.

His emphasis was on the policy needed to address the social aspects of fire management, as well as the operational side. He suggested that good policy on fire would lie somewhere between the two extremes of complete freedom of individual human judgement, and a set of 'rule books' giving precise directions. He pointed out, correctly, that the first extreme would lead, at times, to catastrophe, and the second would never be achievable, given the complexity of the subject.

After giving a list of disastrous fires in California since 1961, Jerry Williams pointed out that the worst losses from these fires occurred where prescribed burning had been withheld, as a matter of political policy. The reasons for this policy were given as visual quality, alleged species conservation, and water catchment values. They resulted in the accumulation of heavy fuel loads, in which fires became uncontrollable, despite California's then annual $3 billion firefighting budget. He suggested that there may even be a tendency for fire-fighting services to encourage the political tendency to foster a fire suppression approach, in preference to that of prevention. Ever bigger budgets lie in that direction. Yet wildfires 'simply outrun' the reliance on more and better equipment, and, in the real world, visual quality, species conservation, and water catchments suffer.

In closing, Dr. Williams called for a better understanding of fire's dynamic role in conserving natural systems, rather than the false view that such systems can be maintained in a static way, by attempted fire exclusion. The dynamic viewpoint would benefit both nature and society. It might be relevant to a recent British fire dispute, which has ecological, social, and economic aspects, of relevance to the Australian bushfire debate.

Toffs and Twitchers

The idea of landscape fires in cold, foggy Britain may be surprising, but there is a long history. William Camden (1551-1623) an English antiquarian, commented on the traditional use of fire by Devon country folk in the sixteenth century.

The English naturalist Gilbert White (1788), in his letters to Thomas Pennant, described large heath fires in Hampshire, which country folk lit to stimulate grass for their cattle. This was despite a statute passed in the reign of William and Mary, which threatened '*whipping and confinement in the house of correction*' for those burning '*grig, ling, heath and furze, goss or fern…*'. More recently, there have been significant fires on heaths in the north of England.

In Britain there has been much debate, some acrimonious, on the effects of fire on heather, in particular in association with the economically important activity of grouse shooting. Such shooting is expensive, and landowners are often wealthy gentry or aristocrats. We may, loosely, call the grouse moor owners '*toffs*', although they are not all aristocrats. I believe one of their number made his fortune out of renovating plebeian public-houses in southern England.

The nuances of the British class system may elude those from other nations, but environmental issues in Britain sometimes have an element of centuries of historical class conflict, for example fox hunting, and rambling along traditional footpaths across private land. I suspect that the dispute over grouse shooting and heather burning has an element of that historical mental baggage, but, as the self-made public house renovator shows, simplistic assumptions can be misleading.

The Moorland Association represents the interests of the landowners, *toffs* or not, who claim to own and manage over 700,000 (over 283,000 hectares) of the estimated 800,000 acres (over 323,000 hectares) of heather in England and Wales.

Early criticism of the management of moorland for grouse came from the Royal Society for the Protection of Birds. A common name for a bird-watcher in England, especially the more earnest ones, is '*twitcher*'. The *twitchers* objected to gamekeepers shooting hawks, to protect the grouse. This brought the *twitchers* into conflict with the *toffs*.

In addition to shooting hawks, or robbing their nests, gamekeepers have also long burned the heather in strips, as soon as it reached the top of their gumboots. This '*muir*' burning became an allied bone of contention, with claims that it was ecologically harmful. In fact, heather depends on fire for regeneration, and grouse depend on young heather for food.

An early book, by a knowledgeable landowner, Lord Lovat, mentioned how fire was important in reducing ticks and worm parasites which could adversely affect grouse health and fecundity. His work was quoted in a later book, by Kozlowski and Ahlgren, where the authors added that parasites on mammals are also reduced by burning. I have already noted the use of fire in Africa and Madagascar to reduce ticks. I can find no research in Australia on this benefit of fire, yet it might well be relevant. Kangaroos, and other Australian native animals, are commonly infested with ticks.

In Britain, the importance of fire to grouse has other aspects. Grouse feed on the young, nutritious tips of heather, so as heather grows taller, the grouse can no longer reach their food. At the same time, grouse need taller heather for shelter from predators such as hawks, so it is important that heather burning leaves patches of older, unburnt heather. This is achieved by burning in strips up the hillsides. If, however, this deliberate burning is neglected, or prevented by poorly informed legislation, an eventual fierce fire will, as at Fylingdales in northern England, burn all the heather in the area, so leaving no refuge, or food, for the grouse.

Taking a cross-disciplinary viewpoint, such fierce heather fires are not entirely bad. The fierce fire at Fylingdales in 2003 burned deep into the soil and peat, and revealed prehistoric archaeology, in the form of carved stones, which may be 3,000 years old. Presumably the peat concealing them has built up over that period. This suggests to me that the recent fire may have burnt deeper than any for the last 3,000 years.

From a long-term, balanced view, it has been pointed out that long past burning may have destroyed the habitat for elk and reindeer in Scotland, but other species, including grouse and hares, have thrived. Not only do grouse benefit from suitable fire frequency and pattern, but red deer are attracted to the better grazing on burnt ground for up to three years after fire.

Ecosystems are complex, and, due to the chaotic and unpredictable nature of some events, there can be diverse outcomes from a disturbance such as fire. Whether those outcomes are 'good' or 'bad' depends on your ethical, economic, or perhaps disciplinary point of view. Outcomes are subject to political judgement and negotiation, as Christian Kull has rightly pointed out. We might also consider that the branch of philosophy known as aesthetics enters into landscape choice, and remember that humans hold very diverse ideas on beauty.

From about the 1980s to the present, the dialectic over *muir* burning and raptor control has continued, mainly between landowners on one side, and the above mentioned two conservationist bodies, English Nature, and the Royal Society for the Protection of Birds, on the other. English Nature lobbied successfully for political prevention of burning, or at least the imposition of such onerous bureaucratic conditions that landowners would find it very difficult to burn. There was also a linked campaign by the Royal Society for the Protection of Birds, against the shooting of raptors by gamekeepers.

The landowners, with their incomes at stake, responded vigorously, countering the claims of English Nature, with evidence from an economist, who quantified the importance of grouse shooting to the Scottish economy, and from a number of natural scientists, who found that burning in a mild, patchy manner had benefits for both grouse and heather. Another source, the Countryside Alliance, source claimed that raptor control is not only beneficial to grouse, but to other birds.

The political outcome was a reversal of the burning regulations, and the decision on when, where, and how to burn returned to the local control of landowners and their game keepers. It seems to me that, in their own economic interests, such people will tend to use fire responsibly. A whole layer of costly bureaucracy was dismantled, and I doubt if the bureaucrats were pleased. English Nature had its legal and financial wings clipped, and was renamed 'Natural England'.

Although the *toffs* seem to be the present winners, the battle continues in the news media, with emotional appeals to conserve raptors. Some articles draw on information from the RSPB. In contradiction, heather burning and grouse management in England are strongly supported by another conservation body, The Heather Trust, which aims to promote sound moorland management. This conservation body points to the loss of 23% of heather moorland in Scotland between the 1940s and 1980s.

One possible outcome is that, if moorland owners cannot manage grouse and heather as long experience tells them to, they will convert the land to other uses, such as sheep grazing, or tree plantations. Landscape is, indeed, a highly negotiable matter.

Summing Up

Noongar people, in south-western Australia, faced the same problems of living off the land, and protecting themselves from the dangers of uncontrollable fire, as humans in other lands. We should not be surprised to find that they used landscape fire in similar ways.

-oOo-

Essay 14

Four More Opinions on Fire

> *'History is philosophy from examples.'*
> Dionysius of Halicarnassus, circa 30 BC

In south-west Australia, over the past few decades, there has been both constructive and misleading debate over past burning by the *Noongar* people. I, and many others, including dozens of *Noongar* Elders I have met, and some eminent humanities scholars I know, or once knew, believe that *Noongars* traditionally used landscape fire judiciously, and frequently, for a number of rather obvious and sensible reasons. These were relevant to human safety, nature conservation for both food and amenity, and bushfire management. Further, *Noongars* greatly enjoyed burning.

Recalling that interesting old man from Halicarnassus, and feeling philosophical and historical, I have browsed some old West Australian newspapers, and found many references to bushfire. These are history, not science, but give a useful cross check on some scientific claims. They are not anecdotal, since they were published. Whether they are apocryphal can best be judged by comparing them with each other, looking for the property of surprising *'consilience'*, as suggested by William Whewell (1794-1866).

The newspaper dates I explored range from the 1840s to the 1950s, but four items, two from the mid-nineteenth century, and two from the mid-twentieth century, drew my particular attention. They are worthy of comparison, and careful thought.

In south-west Australia, there is a broad band of sandy heath, known as *kwongan*, to the east of the Darling Scarp. In January 1845, a West Australian settler called *'Sandy Farmer'*, from east of the Darling Scarp, apparently stung by *'sand groper'* jokes from the rival colony in South Australia, wrote to the *Inquirer* newspaper in Perth about the virtues of sand for farming. One point he made was that *'on the generality of sand the bush-fires will not touch the vegetation* more than once in two years – that which was burnt last year will not burn this year. This description of soil has therefore this advantage – that there is abundance of feed to be found on that portion which was run over by last year's fires, which will remain until the new feed springs up, forced by the ashes of this year's fires.' He was describing a two-phase fire and vegetation mosaic, created by *Noongar* hunters, and potentially useful to shrewd settlers then, and bushfire managers now. There has been quite recent dispute over historic fire frequency in the *kwongan* heath (Essay 21), with some academics, who have used a botanical model, claiming that fire more frequent than ten years would cause the extinction of some plants. Yet might '*Sandy Farmer*' and his practical experience be more reliable than a model created by botanists with little practical experience of bushfire?

A few years later, in the *Inquirer* of June, 1850, a letter appeared from '*A York Settler*'. Those familiar with the history of the small town of York, in Western Australia, may identify him, from his literary style, as Captain Richard Goldsmith Meares, Resident Magistrate at York. He wrote '*I think I may say, without the slightest hesitation, that the country from North to South, and East to West, as far as it is known, has been burned the past summer, more or less, by the natives*'. He went on to describe how *Noongars* would light fires in pursuit of small animals, so burning the native grasses, which were grazing for his sheep. Although the sheep were his, we may question whether the grass belonged to him. Surely he was the trespasser. His use of the phrase '*more or less*' suggests that he saw unburnt patches, but, unlike '*Sandy Farmer*', did not see the advantage of rapid nutrient cycling by frequent mosaic burning on sand.

The settler from York urged the government of the day to banish bushfires, for he argued that '*if the natives are still allowed every summer to fire the country, the sheep will be all starved to death*'. He added '*Now I think it is only fair on our parts – if we deprive the natives of a few kangaroo rats and opossums, which we must do if we prohibit them from burning the country in the summer months – to issue to them a weekly ration of meal, as a compensation for the said animals.*'

He went on that '*There is one more thing which is worthy of notice: the natives must, and will, have fire to cook and sleep by, and the only means they have of carrying fire is by lighting two or three pieces of bark, which they hold in their hand like a torch. Now what can be more dangerous than this in the summer, when the grass and every thing is as dry as tinder; let them be ever so careful, it is almost impossible for them to prevent the bush taking light.*'

As a managerially creative and frugal afterthought, he proposed that '*To prevent this, I would propose that the Government do issue to the head of every aboriginal family one box of matches every month. This, I think, would have great tendency towards stopping the bush-fires, and at a very trifling expense to the Government.*'

I doubt if this last suggestion made much impression on the then Government, or the *Noongars,* if they knew about it. However, if my guess at his identity is correct, the correspondent was a retired officer from a famous British regiment, and a Waterloo veteran to boot, so he probably did have political influence in various ways. His opinion on bushfire had previously been sought by the Governor in 1846, and was taken into consideration in drafting the Bushfire Ordinance passed in 1847, which banned burning by Aborigines, the penalty being public flogging of up to fifty lashes, or imprisonment on Rottnest Island. I doubt if the *Noongars* read the ordinance, since it failed to prevent fires, hence the letter of 1850. If the *Noongars* had read it, or heard of it, we can imagine their anger and disbelief at such an arrogant and brutal law concerning their traditional fire management of their own forest, heath, and grassland. No wonder they look so unhappy in old photographs from the prison on Rottnest Island.

Jumping forward a century to 1950, in the opinion column of *The Daily News*, a correspondent from Crawley, called *'One Who Has Seen',* wrote *'For generations before the white man saw Australia, the aborigines fired the land to obtain food, and prevent future fires. It's a pity that we, with some modern equipment, don't take a lesson from these primitives, and have more controlled burning.'* Apart from the crass use of the word *'primitives'*, he showed some understanding of bushfire. Was he a descendant of an old settler family?

In a fourth example, again in 1950, the *West Australian* newspaper reported that a beekeepers' conference had discussed bushfire policy with a representative of the Forests Department. A beekeeper, Mr. R. Livesey of Denmark, pointed out that *Noongar* people, in their form of husbandry, had included the judicious use of fire, but that the Forests Department at that time did not believe that severe bushfires could be minimised by burning off with light, controlled fires. Quoting thousands of acres of forest severely burnt by wild fires in the previous summer, Mr. Livesey claimed that the Forests Department's fire control policy had failed.

He was contradicted by Mr. A.J. Milesi, then fire control officer of the Forests Department, who blamed the severe fires on careless burning *'by others'*. Some beekeepers supported Mr. Milesi. Nevertheless, the conference agreed to a motion expressing grave concern at the failure of the Forests Department to *'adequately protect forests from uncontrolled bushfires.'* There was no suggestion that beekeepers should be issued with matches at Government expense, but the motion may have helped to encourage a Conservator of Forests, Mr. A.C. Harris, to introduce more deliberate controlled burning. Clearly it was not enough to prevent the disastrous bushfires in 1961 around Dwellingup, and widely elsewhere.

Drawing these four news items together, I get the impression of long standing muddled thinking over bushfire policy in south-west Australia, due initially to a failure by some politically influential early European settlers to understand why *Noongars* burnt the bush frequently, and the likely harmful effect on *Noongars,* settlers, plants, and animals, of preventing such fires.

We should cautiously note that York is far from Augusta and Walpole, and different groups of *Noongars* probably used different methods and timing of burning. For example, I have been told that the *Wadandi* people, along the Blackwood River, did not burn in summer, but in autumn. I don't know if this is true, but it's worth investigating with the *Wadandi* descendants. It might relate to academic conservation claims about some *'rare and endangered'* frogs (*Geocrinia*) in their country, allegedly under threat from prescribed burning. These frogs are found along 'Spearwood Creek', and, as mentioned previously, I have been told, by a late *Noongar* Elder, that spear shaft thickets along creeks were protected from fire for twelve years.

Fire marks on over five hundred old *balga* (grasstree, *Xanthorrhoea preissii*) stems, some dating back to 1750, suggest that most of the *jarrah* forest was burned every two to four years, rather than the biennial burning east of the Darling Scarp. Using the same *balga* technique in the goldfields woodlands near Coolgardie, fire intervals back to the nineteenth century show eight to ten year intervals in goldfields woodland before World War 1. *Balga* stems at Dryandra woodland, on the east side of the *jarrah* forest give old fire intervals of around fifteen years on dry rocky ridges, but only two year intervals along formerly grassy creek banks. The former grassy bank fires are remarkably regular, clearly indicating deliberate human involvement, rather than simply accidents or lightning. The two year intervals are ideal for some formerly abundant native grasses, such as Kangaroo Grass (*Themeda triandra*), and Feather Spear Grass (*Austrostipa elegantissima*). These were surely of interest to *Noongar* people as kangaroo grazing.

What the news items suggest to me is the primary need for West Australian Governments to talk to *Noongar* Elders before future fire policy is made. After all, older *Noongars* still know their country well, and can draw on thousands of years' fire experience, if we are willing to listen patiently, and respectfully, and not allow ourselves to be fooled by shallow and contradictory *'scientism'*.

As mentioned before, in 1840 the English polymath William Whewell suggested a philosophical concept called *'consilience'*. It means a surprising and convincing coming together of information from different sources. It is similar to legal corroboration, and like law is intellectually open not only to science, but also to other kinds of human knowledge, such as history, including the traditional knowledge of Aboriginal people. It is a valuable cross check on the validity of ecological conclusions drawn solely from science, particularly by using statistical models. These can be true, but if false, may lead to poor political bushfire policy, resulting in heavy fuels, uncontrollable fire behaviour, loss of human life and property, and long lasting damage to natural ecosystems.

Professor Whewell was not against science. He himself published scientific papers, and in fact coined the word *'scientist'*. But he knew that truth must be carefully cross checked elsewhere for consilience. Being also a philosopher, he was quite likely influenced by the views of David Hume (1711-1776), who wrote *'Indulge your passion for science ... but let your science be human, and such as may have a direct reference to action and society'*.

Nor should we ever forget Dionysius of Halicarnassus.

-oOo-

Essay 15

This essay first appeared in the international magazine 'Philosophy Now' (Issue 109 Aug/September 2015). It appears here under their terms of publication, with minor changes and additions.

Bushfire, Logic and Ambrose Bierce

> *'What I understand by philosophy is a terrible explosive,*
> *in the presence of which all is in danger.'*
> Friedrich Nietsche, Ecce Homo, 1908.

Those who have not dabbled in philosophy may be unaware of Nietsche's warning. Similarly, those who live in cooler, wetter climates, may be unaware that fire in the landscape, or bushfire, is Australia's most lethal and costly natural hazard, literally a *'terrible explosive'*. Big, uncontrollable bushfires in the recent past have killed millions of trees and wild animals, thousands of farm animals, and some humans too.

Apart from deaths, bushfires incinerate property, such as bridges, farm fencing, homes, and even, a few years ago, an astronomical observatory. The cost to the economy is significant. So bushfire management is, for Australians, no trivial matter. Yet, despite many enquiries since the 1930s, we still have serious bushfires, which seem to be increasing in extent and intensity. Further, we still have some people who claim that pre-emptive burning should be banned, or much reduced.

Australian philosophers should be interested in bushfire epistemology, logic, and ethics. Sources of bushfire knowledge are diverse, including traditional Aboriginal knowledge; historical records from early European settler diaries, letters, and journals; recent scientific research; economics, politics; and law. Logic is needed to arrive at rational policy on bushfire. Although logic may seem to point to a particular solution, we must shun the paths of false logic. Also, there may be ethical objections to some seemingly logical solutions. For example bulldozing all native vegetation might abolish bushfire, but would not be a good idea from many other points of view. Even aesthetics come into the picture. Although many urban Australians, of recent migrant descent, see blackened ground as ugly, Aboriginal people see it as beautiful, and describe it as '*cleaned up*'. Ontology is always useful, to distinguish between what is real, and what is imaginary.

While local volunteers provide most of the weary fire fighters, they are under the ultimate direction of salaried fire officers, who are public servants, wear smart shirts, big hats, many medals, and appear on television, looking worried. Budget and big hats may be central to their thinking. Policy and budget are largely dictated by politicians, who have budgets and metaphorical big hats of their own, and usually appear by helicopter in the aftermath, dispensing sympathy.

It may seem, to some, that Australia has addressed the bushfire bureau-political chain well (especially the hats, medals, helicopters and sympathy), yet there is ongoing dispute over the best way to prevent destructive bushfires. Some, including most farmers and volunteer bushfire fighters, with practical bushfire experience, are in favour of simplification, by returning to something like traditional Aboriginal management, where the bush was deliberately lit at short intervals, in a mosaic pattern, so keeping fuels low, and fires mild, even in summer. Local knowledge is essential for this approach. Those in big hats should play a supporting role, not a supreme directing role. In other words, let's make fire our friend, and use fire to fight fire.

There are many historical accounts of this approach, for example the early German explorer Ludwig Leichardt described frequent mild bushfires in New South Wales in the 1840s, lit by Aborigines. He pointed out that such fires, although widespread and common, were not a threat to humans. Early European farmers imitated Aboriginal burning, to keep themselves safe. More recent bushfires in New South Wales, often in long unburnt areas such as National Parks, have been unmistakeably menacing, due to heavier fuel.

Some natural scientists say that bushfire history is anecdote; or mythology; that little is known about Aboriginal burning; or even that such burning is impossible; and that frequent, mild fires would destroy '*biodiversity*' (however that slippery word may be defined). They say that history is unreliable, and only natural science can lead to the truth about bushfire. I suspect that the philosopher Robin G. Collingwood might have strongly disagreed with that view, since he saw history as an essential part of human understanding.

However, one Australian professor of biology, apparently dismissing history, wrote a letter to the prestigious journal Nature, titled '*Don't Fight*

Fire with Fire'. This may have reinforced his appointment as a bushfire adviser to the New South Wales government, from 1996-2004. In that time there were many uncontrollable bushfires. We should not, of course, allow ourselves to be misled by the old logical error of *post hoc, ergo propter hoc*, but we can still ponder. More recently that professor held an academic appointment in the United Arab Emirates, where I would imagine there are few bushfires. Again, it would be foolish to assume that this situation is due to the professor's onetime presence.

But is natural science the only, and most reliable source of information on bushfire? Statistical induction is a useful tool, but can be misused. Logical blunders have been noticed in refereed natural science journals. Could the broader scope of philosophy help us to get closer to the truth? History, and practical experience, can be astringent cross checks on findings by the scientific method, or a version thereof.

The cynic Ambrose Bierce is not widely acclaimed as a philosopher, yet he did have some useful insights. Before the First World War, in his 'Devil's Dictionary', the cunning old codger defined logic as *'The art of thinking and reasoning in strict accordance with the limitations and incapacities of the human misunderstanding'*. This may dismay learned, studious people like me, who are entranced by our own beamish logic, but we should remember that Ambrose also defined learning as *'The kind of ignorance distinguishing the studious'*.

The perspicacious Ambrose did not stop there. He gave a clear example of a suspect syllogism, in which the statement that sixty men can do a piece of work sixty times as quickly as one man (major premise), followed by the conclusion that one man can dig a post-hole in sixty seconds (minor premise), leads to the unavoidable mathematical conclusion that sixty men can dig a post-hole in one second. If used in politics or law, Aristotle would have called it an *'enthymeme'*. Without benefit of formal philosophy, those who have, at one time or another, actually had a shovel in their hands, will find it clearly questionable.

Similarly, those who have, at one time or another, actually had a fire hose in their hands, breathed smoke up their nostrils, felt the enormous radiant heat of fire in long unburnt fuel, heard the roar, and felt the ground shake as a bushfire goes its merry way, may be perturbed at statements by some, claiming support from statistical evidence, that deliberate, mild burning in cooler weather, to mitigate uncontrollable holocaust bushfires in hot, windy weather, is ineffectual, and harmful to the bush.

Lawyers have their own philosophy, called jurisprudence. Like Ambrose Bierce, some medieval Scottish lawyers may not be recognised as philosophers, but showed perspicacity in taking the Latin verb *reptare* (to crawl or creep) and forming the legal terms *subreption* and *obreption*. These mean, respectively, to crawl under the truth, and to crawl over it; in other words to mislead by telling less than the whole truth, or by telling more than the whole truth. In bushfire debate, we need the truth, the whole truth, and nothing but the truth.

The post-hole syllogism is a clear example of *subreption*, as are some claims made in the bushfire debate. Some papers in refereed journals of ecology may mislead public, and hence political opinion. As an example, reports in the news media, and in refereed papers, describe vegetation as destroyed, without a close definition of that word.

Although they may appear to be dead, many Australian plants are well adapted to bushfire, have bulbs or lignotubers, and resprout readily soon after it. They are no more destroyed, by mild fire, than a garden shrub which is pruned. Other Australian plants need fire, or smoke, in order to flower, or germinate from seed. Words can be deceptive, as philosophers such as Locke, Hobbes and Wittgenstein noted.

With regard to the political aspects of bushfire, Ambrose Bierce had it well covered. He defined politics as a strife of interests masquerading as a contest of principles. The strife of interests includes winning the votes of urban dwellers who are rarely subject to bushfire, yet may have assorted passionate notions about its ecology, perhaps gleaned from television or refereed journals. The contest of principles, in this case, is the ethical duty of care to both nature and human society.

As a former loyal public servant, I won't give Ambrose's cynical definition of the word politician, but it involves the word *eel*. We should remember that dictionaries, even if written by the Devil, can of course be wrong. Let's hope that philosophy can come to the rescue, and that there are at least some worthy Australian politicians, and public servants, who understand that bushfire is Australia's most lethal, costly, and urgent natural hazard, and won't use pseudo-science to wriggle out of their duty of care, or ignore bushfire in the hope that it will go away, or become somebody else's responsibility. Should a basic grasp of philosophy be a requirement for political office? Plato thought so.

Might governments have a Department of Philosophy, to peer deeply into the claims of tendentious lobbyists, no matter how impressive their academic qualifications in natural science, or the length of their publication lists? It's a pity that Ambrose Bierce disappeared in 1914, so isn't here to join the debate on philosophy and bushfire. I hope some from Australia, or other fire prone lands, such as USA, Canada, Africa, and even Europe, will.

-oOo-

Essay 16

Eggzackly

There was an old man of Thermopylae, who never did anything properly;
But they said, 'If you choose to boil eggs in your shoes,
You shall never remain in Thermopylae.'

Edward Lear 1812-1888

Over the past few years, there has been some discussion on the strengths, and weaknesses, of mathematical modelling, particularly in the matter of climate change. Having done a little modelling myself, I am enthusiastic about the value of models in exploring the workings of both nature and society, but I am also wary of elevating models to gospel status, no matter how impressive and fashionable they may seem. Assumptions can be wrong, or relevant facts ignored. Sometimes, like an erstwhile American politician called Rumsfeld, we don't even know what we don't know. We must be wisely sceptical.

Rambling around the worldwide web, I found a site by the interesting Dr. Charles D.H. Williams, of the University of Exeter, in England. In it he describes an impressive mathematical model for calculating how long it will take to boil an egg. Most of us know, of course, from our mums, how long it takes, but the model appears to promise much greater accuracy. However, the honest Dr. Williams admits to overlooking at least one lurking assumption, namely that the boiling will always take place at sea-level. Boiling an egg on a mountain top takes longer. For those entranced by publications in refereed journals, there is a paper on the matter.

Perhaps I suffer from a pathological imagination, an unfortunate ancestral Welsh characteristic, possibly shared by Dr. Williams, but I foresee some ambitious career academics seeking funds to further develop the model for egg boiling in mountainous environments. We must steer between the *scylla* of undercooked eggs (ghastly disease epidemics due to pathogenic bacteria?) and the *charybdis* of hard-boiled eggs (widespread flatulence, leading to runaway global warming?).

News media and political interest will be captured, there will be in-depth interviews, and egg boiling panel discussions on television, with carefully selected audiences. A Minister for Egg Boiling will be appointed, and there must also be a Shadow Minister, rather like the *'big-endians'* and *'little-endians'* in Blefuscu and Lilliput. They will attend important conferences in far-off places, at taxpayers' expense, leaving copious trails of CO2 behind them. Some lightweight, frivolous commentators may speak of Dr. Seuss, and the Butter Battle between the *yooks* and the *zooks*, but they will be omitted from the published proceedings.

We must not joke about this. Dr. Williams points out that, as eggs age, they release CO2, so we are all in danger. Everything links to everything. Should we breed egg-free chooks? And what about Animal Rights? Professor Peter Singer may have views on humans stealing eggs from present day oviparous chooks – er, *Gallus gallus domesticus*. He, and others, may even think that boiling eggs is unethical, given that some eggs contain a viable *foetus*.

We need further modelling, and the United Nations should convene an International Panel on Egg Boiling (IPEB). I am available as chair, given a suitable United Nations tax free salary, and copious free first class air travel to attend conferences, and stay in five-star hotels. I may send a copy of this essay to Cluckingham Palace, for the urgent attention of Prince Charles.

-oOo-

Essay 17

Parachute Science & Prescribed Burning

'Some circumstantial evidence is very strong, as when you find a trout in the milk'.
Henry David Thoreau, 1850

It has come to my notice that two medical experts, Professors Smith and Pell of Cambridge University, have submitted to the British Medical Journal an interesting systematic review of the use of parachutes to prevent death and major trauma related to gravitational challenge. They found that there was no experimental, evidence based support for their use. As a former member of the Parachute Regiment, may I urge former colleagues not to abandon use of parachutes, even if some eminent, possibly mischievous medical experts, say that there is no experimental evidence to support their effectiveness. As a matter of practical experience, I remember a trooper of our battalion, in the nineteen fifties, whose main and reserve canopies both failed.

On a similar line of thought to Professors Smith and Pell, a letter to the Canberra Times (December 2006), by Professor Brendan Mackey of ANU, suggested, if I read it correctly, that there is no experimental, evidence based support for the use of widespread prescribed burning to prevent large, lethal bushfires. A similar scornful view of prescribed burning, citing support from *'most authorities'*, was expressed a few years earlier by Professor Robert Whelan, of Wollongong University, in a letter to the prominent scientific journal *Nature*. I don't know who Professor Whelan would regard as *'authorities'*. We may well differ on that point. Both these letters were, of course, written before the last severe bushfires (2019) in south-eastern Australia.

Professors Smith and Pell, the authors of the parachute review, proposed that those who demand rigorous evidence from randomised, controlled parachute experiments should themselves volunteer as a control group, without parachute treatment.

This is a bit extreme, but may I propose that those who, like Professors Mackey and Whelan, are opposed to widespread prescribed burning, should volunteer as a control group, to stand in long unburnt bush, on a hot day, as a fire approaches. An escape track would, of course, be provided through the dense sticks and litter. They should, if still able, publish their observations in a prestigious refereed journal, perhaps *Nature*. They should also encourage the ABC to televise the experiment, with the tense rhetoric and alarming musical embellishment at which their people are so skilled.

It may be worth remembering, with great regret, that the former West Australian Forests Department inadvertently carried out such a trial in January 1958. Some forest workmen were sent, in hot weather, to a bushfire in long unburnt forest near Nannup, in south-west Australia. Four of them, George McCorkhill, Jan Hillier, Robert Johnston, and John Wiltshire-Butler were killed, due to an unexpected wind change, and the ferocity of the fire in long unburnt *jarrah* and *karri* forest. One of the witnesses at the ensuing enquiry described the forest as '*dirty*', a term used by both *Noongar* people and firefighters to describe long unburnt bush, which is liable to burn fiercely in hot, windy conditions. Last time I was in that vicinity I saw a small, sad plaque in memory of the four, outside the former Forests Department office. I believe some forest blocks are named after them, and there may be family members still living in the area.

Such poignant fire history can be valuable as a check on a reported academic claim, by Associate Professor Philip Zylstra, from Curtin University, that withholding fire from south-west forests, such as *karri*, will make them less flammable, because the leaf litter will decompose, leaving a clean floor.

The last time I walked through long unburnt *karri* forest near the south coast, I found it exhausting, due to metre deep stick litter, draped with bark and dead leaves. An ideal recipe for uncontrollable fire in hot, dry, windy weather. I know, because I have fought a couple of such fires, and taken part in over a hundred experimental fires, most in long unburnt *karri* country. During one of these, I was still clearing an escape path through two metre high Prickly Moses bush, when, due to a misunderstanding, someone lit the experimental fire at the centre of the plot. Due to my vigorous use of a sharp bill hook, I escaped and survived, just as in the army I survived jumping out of various airplanes due to wearing a parachute.

I wonder how much practical experience Professors Mackey and Whelan have had of bushfire?

-oOo-

Essay 18

Violins and Vico

> *'Verum et ipsum factum convertuntur'.*
> *Giovanni Battista Vico 1710, De Italorum Sapientia*

In south-west Australia, bushfire is managed by the Department of Fire and Emergency Services (DFES); the politically named Department of Biodiversity, Conservation and Attractions (DBCA); and Volunteer Bushfire Brigades. These all base their management on practical methods developed by the former West Australian Forests Department, mainly between 1950 and 1980, and by such largely unsung pioneers as Alan McArthur of ANU Forestry School, Phil Cheney and Dave Packham of CSIRO, Rick Sneeuwjagt AFSM, and the late George Peet OAM of the West Australian Forests Department. So what have violins and an eighteenth century Italian philosopher got to do with foresters, scientists, and bushfire? Well, quite a lot actually.

A long time ago, Aristotle suggested that the best way to learn something is to do it. He probably got the idea from Plato, who distinguished between theoretical learning (*episteme*), learning by practical experience (*gnosis*), and general chit-chat (*doxa*).

Giovanni Battista Vico, known to his friends as Giambattista, was an eighteenth century humanist philosopher, no doubt familiar with the ideas of Aristotle and Plato. Although Giambattista was a native of Naples, we may suspect, from his use of the following metaphor, that he had travelled north to the city of Cremona. That city is still famous for its violin makers. He noted that if someone pulled a violin apart, they would learn something about violins. However, if they were to rebuild the violin correctly, they would learn much more. I would add that if they could then play a tune, so much the better. Learning by doing, making, and using something, for example bushfire, can be more direct and valuable than simply abstract chains of what is thought to be true, and even supported by statistical analysis, but if based on false assumptions, can be misleading nonsense.

Giambattista's *'verum factum'* principle is well-known to philosophers, but not so well-known to natural scientists. It is difficult to translate exactly into English. One difficulty is that there is not always a precise mapping between words from different languages, nor to the thinking processes behind them. A cautious attempt at translation is that *'understanding the truth of something, and making, or doing it, are much the same thing'*.

In Cremona today, students of violin making have to pass theoretical exams, but can only graduate once they have actually made a violin. Vico did not deny the value of logic, but he opposed its mechanistic use, and understood that there is far more to human intelligence and practical experience than just linear logic. As noted in a previous essay, the eighteenth century French philosopher, Voltaire, once suggested that an obsession with logic is a sure sign of stupidity. He ridiculed such obsession in his famous novel *Candide*. He might have hit the nail on the head.

Some present day natural scientists pride themselves on their logic, yet are sometimes prone to simplistic scientism, seeing the computer model, statistical software, and the refereed and published paper as the only three fountains of truth, or perhaps the three main rungs on the academic career ladder. They need to ponder the matter of logic more deeply. In my view, every published use of inductive statistics should be accompanied by a three line syllogism (Essay 15) in plain words, so that referees and readers can consider what assumptions the author has made; those that are right; those that are wrong; and those that might have been relevant, but have been missed out altogether.

In the field of bushfire research, might actually doing something often give us a deeper, sounder knowledge than the current academic approach, where professors seem sometimes to be appointed on the basis of a long publication list, regardless of the quality of those publications, or their writers' practical experience? When foresters were responsible for managing bushfire, they learnt much about bushfire by using it, yet, unfortunately, were sometimes not encouraged to publish their knowledge.

Having no computers, software, or scientific journals, *Noongar* people, and other Aboriginal people throughout Australia, managed fire by making and doing, so developing a deep working understanding. They had to, to avoid being burnt to death, or starving. They recognised fire as both a friend, and a potential enemy. Mainly through urban ignorance, we recent arrivals have, at least in south-west Australia, largely destroyed the bushfire violins made by *Noongar* people, thousands of years ago. Today, bushfire can, with luck, or vast expenditure on machines and staff, be deliberately excluded for a while from an area of south-west Australian bush which would, without deliberate fire exclusion, be capable of burning. In some National Parks and Reserves in south-west Australia, such deliberate fire exclusion has been applied in the niftily named 'No Planned Burn Areas, based on questionable ecological claims by some academic botanists and zoologists. The result has been some highly destructive fires, in fuel loads of up to fifty tonnes per hectare.

Such fierce fires climb into the tree crowns, and destroy any previous finer grained vegetation mosaic, together with its diversity of animals, and other life forms. Restoration of that diverse, fine grained mosaic, or one similar, can only be achieved and maintained by deliberate, and intelligent use of fire, drawing on practical experience.

However, in current heavy fuels, to reintroduce regular, patchy burning, similar to that which was used by *Noongars* long before Europeans arrived, is not a simple matter. As Professor Stephen Pyne of Arizona has well said, fire is not an *'ecological pixie dust'*, to be sprinkled willy-nilly. We need reliable scientific information, but we also need better to understand the long history of human fire use. This is best achieved by reading relevant history, and using fire ourselves in a careful, exploratory way. I am sure Aboriginal people can draw on traditional knowledge, perhaps included in 'songlines' (Essay 1).

Following fierce forest fires in preceding decades, foresters in the 1950s tried to reproduce the frequency of *Noongar* burning, which they then well knew was every 3-4 years in the *jarrah* forest. They did not, however, understand the ecological subtlety of the *Noongar* approach. Also, they found the work load too much, and simplistically doubled it to 6-8 year intervals. This was better than no burning at all, but was done in ignorance of the importance of fine grained mosaics, created and maintained by frequent fire, and the stabilising effect of such mosaics on fire behaviour. Even fire in 6-8 year old litter can get out of control in extreme summer conditions. Embarrassing escapes from 'controlled' burns have occurred.

I once met a *Noongar* Elder at Goomalling, who, as far as I can remember, called such escapes *'karla koombariny'* (big fire?), and he regarded them as a very bad thing. My informant spoke these *Noongar* words quite fast, so I hope I heard them correctly. I invite advice on this from *Noongar* speakers. Part of the traditional role of a *bridya* (traditional fire boss) was to safeguard against such damaging fires.

Despite my occasionally sceptical view of mathematical modelling, a good and prestigious American mathematician, Craig Loehle, has used Percolation Theory in a competent and useful way to show that maintaining a mosaic of patches burnt at various times in the past can make an area proof against destructive fires. He describes the idea as similar to that of bulkheads on ships to prevent flooding after an accident. In his paper he points out that *'a threshold of burning exists at which a landscape becomes essentially fireproof'*, and that it *'reduces the acreage that must be treated to achieve a fireproof condition.'*

In times of tight budgets, fire managers might consider this option of frugal, yet effective, patchy fuel reduction burning. It appears to be very similar to patchy burning by *Noongar* people, not to mention the original inhabitants of India, Burma, North America, South America, Africa, the Middle East, and even Europe (Essay 13)

Even if a perfect facsimile of traditional *Noongar* burning is not achieved, much may be learnt from doing the practical exercise in south-west Australia. If approached in a tactful manner, with a willingness to listen, *Noongar* Elders can, I am sure, offer much valuable advice. If successful, the final outcome will be more stable, more diverse, more predictable, and less dangerous than a simplified, unstable fire regime, in which giant patches can burn fiercely, and dangerously, at often long, but unpredictable, intervals. It should also be faster and cheaper than fighting unpredictable wildfires. If unsuccessful, we are at liberty to try other methods, until we get it right. I believe some management experts call this 'adaptive management'.

Bidi Burning

According to Kooda Cornwall, a well-known *Noongar* and employee of the former Department of Conservation and Land Management (CALM), an individual *Noongar* track was called a *bidi*, with the plural form of *bidi-bidi*. Major *bidi-bidi* are shown on a map drawn by Dr Noel Nannup, another well-known and respected *Noongar* Elder who worked for CALM, and I believe *bidi-bidi* still have great significance to *Noongar* people, since they are intimately entwined not only with fire, but also with history, spiritual matters, family territory (*moort boodja*), and land custodianship.

I have previously mentioned that the word *bidi* may also be used for veins and arteries. Is there, in *Noongar* minds, a deep metaphorical relationship between branched and spreading bush tracks; the internal circulation of blood; and the water drainage system of their *boodja*? Being made by, and for walking, *bidi-bidi* must have harmonised with the natural topography and drainage systems, but tracks built for locomotives, or motor vehicles often ignore them.

The same use of tracks, or songlines, to define territory is known from other parts of Australia. It is a distinctive feature of some Aboriginal paintings. The relevance of songlines to bushfire management has been suggested by the world's best fire historian, Professor Stephen Pyne of Arizona. One song could contain vital information on geography, climate, plants and animals, sacred sites, creeks, water holes, camping sites, history etc. In other words, the full 'Human Ecology' of an area.

On that matter, there are two recreational walk tracks maintained by the

93

DBCA. One is called *Munda Bidi*, the other the *Bibbulmun* Track[1]. Both these tracks offer a clear opportunity to test the *bidi* burning technique. The benefits would be greater security for walkers; protection of overnight huts and wooden bridges; greater diversity of habitat for native plants and animals along the track; better flowering and seed germination, and decreased possibility of the DBCA facing legal action for injury, or loss of life, due to a major bushfire. Maybe some present day *Noongar* people still know the songs for the *bidi-bidi*, or could create new ones. I think tourists would be happy to pay for a guide to show them along the track, sing the song, and explain its meaning. This would create employment, and raise the international profile of *Noongar* culture. I suspect that songlines, dance, and art could be used to create burning demonstrations by *Noongar* people for tourists, perhaps initially in National Parks or on private property (Essay 19). Entrance fees would be paid, but, under present heavy fuels, some of the initial income would be needed for site preparation and support from DFES and DBCA fire crews. Political understanding and backing would be needed for such support.

An uncontrollable fire in the long-unburnt Mount Cooke area in 2003 burnt a walkers' hut on the *Bibbulmun* Track. Luckily, nobody was in it at the time, but government departments, having a duty of care, should not trust to luck. Apart from walk tracks, *bidi* burning may be found useful in burning small nature reserves; areas of critical habitat; small patches of bush on private property; and road verges. There are many violins to make.

Translating the geometry to a field situation, we can, in a relatively small area, use rakes, brush-cutters, or leaf blowers, to create a set of wandering *bidi-bidi*, crossing each other to form a network. As areas get bigger, the physical labour of creating such paths, especially in long unburnt fuel, will be prohibitive. Bigger areas, perhaps long unburnt, will need machines, such as bobcats or quad bikes. In some places close to towns, teenagers could be encouraged to create tracks for trail or mountain bikes.

There may be opposition to this youthful approach from those with certain social views, but the greater useful effect in preventing uncontrollable blazes must be considered. Potential dieback (*Phytophthora*) spread must also be borne in mind, but this is a factor in any form of prescribed burning. As an historical note, it is known, from former Forests Department reports, that hundreds of miles of such tracks, as firebreaks, were created in the 1920s, using a horse drawn scraper made of two pieces of railway line, welded together at sixty degrees. I wish they had thought of

---

[1] I am not sure about the validity of this name. As I understand it, the *Bibbulmun* were, and still are, a *Noongar* group who live further south, so DBCA might need to rename it.

weaving such tracks into a more effective network.

More recently *bidi-bidi* were created, and burnt, near the Bridgetown fire station. Using an industrial back-pack blower, in three year old *jarrah/marri* fuel, the paths were constructed, in early spring, at normal walking pace. An area can be sub-divided as finely as needed, or as practically possible, or within the constraints of a particular budget and time available. In mild weather, such as the West Australian winter, *bidi-bidi* can be more easily created by burning in fine spells, using drip-torches. Natural bare areas, such as rocks, water bodies, or existing kangaroo paths may be included in the pattern. After *bidi-bidi* creation, and before burning, it has been noted, from fresh droppings, that kangaroos seem delighted to use such clear paths.

If fuels are initially heavy, the patches might need initial edge burning in mild weather, to avoid spread into adjacent patches. Once sufficient fuel reduction is achieved over the whole area, then fires can be lit, even in summer, without causing major problems. Dr Ian Abbott has shown, beyond reasonable doubt, from historical information, that most *Noongar* burning was done in summer, and his findings match well with the letters from the early days of European settlement (Essay 6). It must, therefore, have been in much lighter fuel than is now common. Without strong convection and ember spread from heavy fuel, each burnable patch was quarantined by neighbouring unburnable patches, and, given low fuel in the burning patch, the fire was mild, regardless of ambient air temperature and fuel dryness.

If, due to past long fire exclusion, fuels are initially dangerously heavy, it will be hard work at first. Thoughtful working with natural features, such as topography, drainage, creeks, and rock outcrops, will be needed. As fuels become lighter, and the cycle becomes established, it will become much easier. Only occasional hand-beating of straying fires will be needed, as described by Captain John Lort Stokes of HMS Beagle in 1840, or Forester Brockway at Mundaring in the nineteen twenties. Early settlers learnt, most likely from *Noongar* fire managers, that *marri* saplings make the best beaters. They have bigger leaves, and a *jarrah* branch, even if green, can burst into flames almost immediately it is put near flame.

If patches are not burnt as soon as they are ready to carry fire, then there will be an eventual, and inevitable, loss of mosaic stability, due to fuel flammability in adjacent patches, and wide spread of the fire. This will result in a coarser mosaic, that is to say, a loss of vegetation diversity. In other words, the mosaic will self-organise in response to a decreased ignition frequency. This increase in patch size and fire intensity will be independent of, and additional to, any potential change in fire behaviour blamed on climate change.

Restoring Mosaics in Larger Areas

In larger areas, such as National Parks and State Forests, mosaics could be restored by using the above method, combined with the current careful, broadscale, aerial bombing by the DBCA, using knowledge of different drying rates connected with different vegetation, aspect, topography, soil type, and season.

For example, in south-western Australia some sedge swamps can burn even in winter, given enough wind. The flames move through the sedges, over the standing water underneath. This prevents deep burning of peat, which occurs especially in autumn fires, and causes alarm in some ecologists (Essay 19). At the same time, the water is given a good smoking, which can result in spectacular germination of some native flowers, including the delightful Brown Boronia, in the following spring. The importance of smoke to seed germination was first discovered in South Africa by De Lange and Boucher. Their work was, a few years later, unsurprisingly found to apply in south-west Australia.

Ridge tops and north facing slopes in the *jarrah* forest are usually dry enough to burn in spring, valleys and south facing slopes only later. By judicious lighting, perhaps by incendiary capsules from fixed wing aircraft, perhaps from helicopters, large areas can be burnt patchily, and economically, provided intervals between fires are not too long.

Burning of such large areas does, however, create relatively coarse mosaics. There are advantages in creating finer grained mosaics, by preceding aerial burning with hand burning along creeks using small scale *bidi-bidi*. For example, small marsupials, known to *Noongars* as *quokka*, shelter from predators in dense thickets along creeks. At the same time, they need recently burnt vegetation nearby, to provide food. A fine grained mosaic of burns would be of advantage to these threatened populations. Since *quokka*, and other small to medium mammals, were hunted and eaten by *Noongar* people, it seems likely that areas along creeks were burnt as a fine grained mosaic. According to one Elder, some creeks were habitually burnt on one side only, then the other side a year or two later, so providing shelter and feed close to each other.

A *Noongar* technique used to hunt larger animals in thickets has been described by Dr Neville Green. Fire breaks were created by treading down the surrounding shrubs, and small patches were burnt. Kangaroos and wallabies got their legs tangled as they fled the fire, and so were easily speared or clubbed. We may be able to recreate similar patchy habitat, offering both shelter, and fresh shoots for food, by careful *bidi* burning, without, of course, the accompanying slaughter. In Rosemary Whitehurst's

Noongar dictionary I have noted the term '*naariny marlark*', which I believe means 'thicket burning'

At the same time, if such fine mosaics increased animal populations, culling might be necessary from time to time, to prevent overpopulation, disease, and habitat degradation. Who better to do the culling than *Noongar* people? The need for such culling should provoke some deeper thinking about the meaning of the word 'conservation' in the real world, and would be in line with the requirement for National Parks to allow *Noongar* traditional activities.

Creating Mosaics within Mosaics

Bushfire mosaics have a nested property, in that each patch labelled as 'burnt', can, in reality, be itself a mosaic of second order burnt and unburnt, due to the presence of rocks, or moist, shady places, different aspects, animal diggings etc. This second order mosaic will be most pronounced when fires are frequent and mild, in low fuel. It will disappear when long fire exclusion and heavy fuel loads create large, fierce fires, which coarsen and simplify mosaics.

A good example of such total burnout, due to heavy, connected fuel, was the already mentioned fire at Mt. Cooke, just east of Wungong Catchment. After that fire, some *balga* grasstrees cleaned near Mt. Cooke, around the source of the Canning River, showed a history of frequent burning (2-4 years) before the 1920s, and back into the nineteenth century. There have been other fires, notably in National Parks, where long fire exclusion has been attempted, based on questionable advice.

Due to a policy of attempted fire exclusion, the bushland in King's Park, Perth, often has heavy, connected fuel, and has been damaged by three fierce fires since 1980. Overseas, in 1988, Yellowstone National Park in Wyoming burned fiercely, due to attempted broadscale fire exclusion. In South Africa, Kruger National Park burned fiercely in 2001, for the same reason, with loss of both human and animal life.

In restoring mosaics, anomalous patches will be found, which will not carry a fire as often as the surrounding country. They can be safely left unburnt, provided that they are quarantined by a frequently burnt matrix. Fire sensitive plants and animals will benefit.

The DBCA has already tried ecological mosaic burns in the southern jarrah forest, and have found that a plant species botanists believed was endangered by frequent burning, actually increased fourfold when frequently burnt, due to the mosaic refuge effect. My understanding is that DBCA are trying to repeat this using aircraft, and incendiary bombs, and are guided by seasonal moisture gradients. I predict that *bidi* burning by people on the ground will be needed to achieve a finer grained mosaic in some places, especially along creeks.

Conclusions

There are both aesthetic and spiritual aspects to fire. *Noongar* people often describe recently burnt country as 'cleaned up'. Perhaps they are referring to aesthetic or spiritual matters, as well as the physical. Only they can tell us.

The geometry of '*bidi* burning' might serve these purposes. Bushfire can be a good and friendly spirit, or a bad and hostile one. It can be ugly or beautiful - it depends on us. Due to heavy, neglected fuels, today's bushfires are often bad and hostile, but we can restore a friendly fire regime in south-west Australia, by learning about, and importantly practising, the fire regime practised for thousands of years by *Noongar* people. I hope *Noongar* Elders will help the general public to understand this, and there are certainly skilled artists in the *Noongar* community who could communicate the matter beautifully in pictures.

At the community scale, there is an important role for Local Government, using Volunteer Bushfire Brigades, backed up by bushfire experts from DBCA and FESA. *Bidi* burning can be used around human settlements, in small reserves, or on road verges, but it must not drown in a sea of bureaucratic form-filling. In jarrah and marri forest, regular burning in 2-4 year old litter will make things much safer. Local knowledge is valuable. In National Parks and State Forests, the DBCA can use paid staff, including *Noongar*s, to apply *bidi* burning to conserve plant and animal refuges within areas destined for large aircraft burns.

There are some good young minds in universities, DBCA, and DFES. They should free themselves from tendentious scientism. They have an opportunity to explore the rich interactions between the human mind, human spirit, human history, and natural science. Importantly, they have the staff and budget to actually make violins, which can then be played by fire practitioners.

With regard to written communication, they might do well to start by reading an entertaining essay in the reputable journal Oikos, written by a leading Danish scientist, Kaj Sand-Jensen. From various visits to Denmark, I appreciate the Danish sense of humour. He offers sage advice on how to write consistently boring scientific papers.

-oOo-

Essay 19

Peering into the Future of Bushfire

> *'I never think of the future. It comes soon enough.'*
> Attributed to Albert Einstein, 1930

Yet thinking about the future is not a waste of time. Fire management is an area where there is a definite need for some structured thought about the future, shall we say some foresight? One of the main objectives of fire management in south-west Australia is to protect human life and property from fire, both now and into the future. The other is to conserve wild ecosystems. Both the Department of Biodiversity, Conservation and Attractions (DBCA) and the Department of Fire and Emergency Services (DFES) may benefit from some detailed, professional scenario writing to aid in their planning.

Scenarios may also help them to choose between opposing opinions offered by some academics, which may lead to very different future outcomes. As a start, below are two amateur sketch scenarios by me about fire, based on a perspective starting in the 2030s. I am sure these scenarios can be improved by more skilful writers.

A Constructive Bushfire Scenario

The close association of Aboriginal people with land has been officially recognized in Western Australia. A draft policy statement by the former Department of Conservation and Land Management (CALM) gave amendments to the CALM Act which *'acknowledge Aboriginal interests in national parks, conservation parks, state forest, marine parks and other conservation reserves, including the desire to protect heritage values, be consulted in management, recognise rights for hunting and other traditional activities associated with native title.'* The term *'traditional activities'* includes, obviously, the traditional use of fire to maintain land and vegetation in the condition which traditional owners in the past saw as being to their benefit.

Further, Section 7.3 directed that CALM would seek the introduction of the Biodiversity Conservation Bill to repeal and replace the Wildlife Conservation Act 1950. It was directed that the Biodiversity Conservation Bill should contain provisions that *'enable Aboriginal people to exercise traditional laws and customs.'* Again, it is clear from history that *'customs'* include traditional burning, a custom which was central to *Noongar* culture. A *Noongar* writer, Glenn Kelly, has pointed out that *'Karl (fire) is at the very heart of our culture.'*

Suppose, by the year 2030 the DBCA (or its oft renamed successor) had made effective moves to encourage *Noongar* people to exercise traditional laws and customs, including traditional burning, in National Parks. In the case of John Forrest National Park, this meant involving local *Noongar* people, with family links to the park area, in an attempt to relearn and reintroduce traditional burning. Some scientists were interested in being involved, for example a botanist, who had a particular interest in the restoration and conservation of native grasses, wanted to see if a traditional (2-3 year) burning regime on the clay valley bottoms and scarp face would restore attractive native grasses such as Kangaroo Grass (*Themeda triandra*).

A need was also seen for DBCA resources to be directed toward a public education program, recommended decades earlier in a previous government report by a politician and two eminent fire scientists. This education program would make suburban people more aware of the fire issue, and give them the plain choice between small amounts of smoke from small, planned fires, and very large amounts of smoke, and the danger of losing their houses, from large, unplanned fires. It was also necessary to counter some of the misinformation on the ecological implications of fire. It was clearly explained to the public, and some conservation groups, that appropriate burning is needed to maintain the health and diversity of the vegetation. The prevalence of rot and termite attack on long unburnt *balgas* in the park, and the blatantly unhealthy condition of long unburnt *djiridji* (zamias), were used as clear, practical illustrations of the effects of inappropriate fire exclusion.

The very different impacts on native animals of small, frequent fires, and large, infrequent ones were also clearly explained, with photographs of the many native animals killed by former large, fierce, unplanned fires in other national parks, such as Two People Bay, and Nuyt's Wilderness.

Given the above public education program, and starting carefully, with small fires in cool weather, *bidi-bidi* were established, and the fuel loadings were reduced to the point where burning in summer could be attempted.

100

To do this it was necessary to amend the Bushfires Act.

Using the topography, and predictable wind directions and changes, spot fires (not line fires, for reasons clear to those who understand fire behaviour) were lit near creeks, in suitable weather, and allowed to burn narrow strips up the hillsides. In this way, fires were kept small and controllable, without danger of a wide fire front developing, which would lead to a dangerous escalation of fire behaviour. Usually, the back and flank fires went out, leaving only small head fires to cut their way uphill with the wind. If a flank or backfire developed, it was quickly suppressed. Such fires are known to some as 'finger fires'. Having a long perimeter in relation to their area, these strips of burnt vegetation were favourable to native animals. While the burnt ground gave, in the following winter, the benefits of fresh, nutritious plant growth, the animals were never far from the shelter of unburnt ground.

The head fire flames in such fires were at an acute angle to the ground surface, and so there was greater transfer of radiant heat and smoke into the surface soil than with back fire flames, which either died out, or were at an obtuse angle to the ground behind the fire. Provided that the fire was not in very heavy fuel, and so fierce enough to destroy the seed bank, the acute angle was likely to lead to better germination of seeds. There is a need for research into the different effects of head and back fires on germination. I have seen, in *karri* forest, the massive germination of a patch of *karri* hazel (*Trymalium spathulatum*) seeds in the winter following a summer fire, in which a gust of wind flattened some the headfire flames, at an acute angle, close to the ground, and forced the smoke downwards for a matter of seconds. The seeds germinated thickly only where the wind gust flattened the flames. Elsewhere there was only sparse germination.

Another point to consider with uphill burning is that rock outcrops, which are common in parts of John Forrest National Park, will block '*finger fires*', leaving an unburnt patch on the uphill side, where fire sensitive plants and animals, can survive. The practice of burning downhill does not leave such unburnt patches, and may harm those plants and animals which need them.

Once the big areas of continuous heavy fuel (former 'no planned burn areas') had been broken up into small areas by *bidi-bidi* and strip fires, then areas were burnt out by a mosaic of strip fires, at three to four year intervals on the ridges, and two year intervals in the valleys. This sort of burning was, at the outset, expensive, due to the need for fire crews in attendance while there were still heavy fuels present. However, as the frequent burning began to cover the whole area, the task became easier. There was a need for a serious, not cosmetic commitment by DBCA, and hence ultimately by the

State Government. Aboriginal pressure groups enforced the legal provisions quoted above, and funds were made available by the Federal Government as part of both its reconciliation and environmental programs.

Initially, a problem was encountered with the proliferation of exotic weeds, such as the South African *Watsonia,* from frequent burning, but it was soon found that the *Watsonia* patches stabilised, since not all parts of the landscape are equally suitable for it. Experiments were set up to see if burning at a particular season, or frequency, or in a certain direction, would prove unfavourable to the weed. There were clear precedents in the South African scientific literature of using a combination of appropriate fire, and grazing by native animals, to promote native grasses over time, so pushing out exotics.

The traditional burning became a tourist attraction, integrated with other *Noongar* activities, such as dancing, building *mia-mia* (huts), tool making, and the reestablishment of ancestral *bidi-bidi* tracks. The skilful guiding of the strip fires up the valley sides was an unusual and spectacular sight for tourists. Money raised from tourism led, eventually, to the building of a *Noongar* cultural and historical centre in the park, giving access to a web of educational *bidi-bidi.* Even universities became involved.

A Destructive Bushfire Scenario

Suppose that no moves toward *Noongar* fire involvement were taken. Instead, in the 2030s, under pressure from urban electorates, the West Australian Government adopted a policy of total fire exclusion in National Parks, including the John Forrest National Park. What would be the realistic outcomes, both for nature and humans?

Imagine that, early one summer morning, the Ranger-in-Charge at John Forrest National Park heard, on the radio, the weather forecast for the day. It was the middle of January, and a high pressure cell was situated in the Great Australian Bight, with a trough down the south west coastline. The winds were easterly at about 20 km/hr, and the forecast maximum temperature for the day was 38 degrees Celsius, with 20% humidity.

At morning tea break, the Ranger received a telephone call from the Duty Officer at the DBCA, telling him that a fire was approaching John Forrest National Park from the north-east, on the south side of the Toodyay Road. It was moving rapidly through grass fuels on private property, and was only two kilometres from the eastern boundary of the National Park. Bushfire Service Volunteers were trying to contain the fire, but were short handed, since it was a weekday, and most volunteers were unavailable due to work commitments. No DBCA fire crews were available to help, since they were already busy attending other fires in State Forest. Besides, DBCA fire staff had been '*down sized*' to the point where only a few trained crews were available, with few experienced officers to lead them.

DFES crews were unavailable, since they were concentrating on the defence of suburban housing on the south east boundary of the National Park. With a forecast of the wind backing more toward north east, and strengthening during the day, they saw human life and property as their priorities.

Due to field staff cuts, the Ranger-in-Charge had only one other ranger on duty, and one available on call. Neither staff member had much experience in fire fighting, as there had been little precautionary burning in National Parks for decades. Their only equipment was a 'Fast Attack' vehicle, that is to say a utility with a small, 600 litre tank of water, a pump, and a hose. Pumping at full pressure, the tank would be empty in a matter of minutes. They had hand tools, such as shovels and rake hoes.

The Ranger-in-Charge decided to patrol the eastern boundary, and try to make radio contact with the Bush Fire Volunteers, who had set up a Control Point on the north side of the Toodyay Road. As he and his crewman moved off from the office, they could see in the north-east the white smoke column typical of a fire in light fuel, such as grass.

As the rangers travelled east along a track beside Jane Brook, approaching the eastern boundary, they made radio contact with the Control Point, and informed them of their intention to patrol that boundary. The Incident Controller warned them that the fire was moving fast, and his crews had fallen back to the Toodyay Road.

Moving northwards along the boundary track, the rangers could see the flames racing through the grass on the adjoining private property, and realized that the five metre fire break along the boundary had no hope of stopping the fire, which was throwing embers.

They decided to move away from the boundary, onto a parallel track about a hundred metres inside the park. This track was narrow, with few places where they could turn around. For years, little money had been available for track maintenance. To go off the track meant becoming bogged in dry, sandy gravel. As they moved northwards, the fire itself was concealed from them by a ridge, but there was an ominous change in the colour of the smoke, from white, to black with coppery tints. They knew that the fire had crossed the park boundary, and was now burning in heavy jarrah/marri litter which has not been burnt for over thirty years. The area had been designated, largely on botanical advice, as '*no planned burn*', and was carrying fuel of about 30 tonnes per hectare. A fire in such fuel, in extreme weather conditions, can have flames at least 12 metres high, and a heat output of about 5,000 kilowatts for each metre of fire front. The radiant heat can be enough to ignite bark, blister vehicle paint, or kill an animal, or human, some metres away. Such fires are unstoppable in extreme summer conditions, even with the help of bulldozers and water bombers.

By now, the wind had, as forecast, backed to north-east, and strengthened to 28 km/hr. What was, up to then, the southern flank of the fire, suddenly became a head fire, 200 metres wide, roaring up the slope toward the rangers, who were trapped in the *'dead man zone'*, well-known to trained bush fire fighters. As they came over the ridge, they were blinded by dense, black smoke. Whole *jarrah* trees were on fire, from base to tip, with the crowns exploding as an envelope of terpene gas from volatile eucalyptus oil ignited. The rangers knew that they were in danger, but in trying to turn around, their vehicle was bogged. Remembering their brief fire training, they resisted the urge to get out and run, staying instead inside the cab, with the windows closed.

Due, however, to the ferocity of the fire in long unburnt litter fuel, and the fact that the vehicle was not, for economic reasons, equipped with external spray bars, the approaching fire emitted enormous radiant heat through the windscreen and door panels. This caused the plastic trim inside the cab to give off noxious gases. The occupants tried to defend themselves from the searing radiant heat by holding up their jackets, but, before the windscreen burst from the heat, they were forced by the choking plastic fumes to bail out. Both men died close to the vehicle. A search party later found the blackened shell of the vehicle, flames still flickering around the remains of the tyres, and the charred remains of the occupants, in the typical pugilistic attitude adopted by those who die in agony from fire. It appeared, from their positions, that they had been trying to take refuge under the vehicle.

The fire continued, unstoppable, for the rest of the day. In the heavy fuels, water bombers were of no avail, their water being mostly blown away by the strong wind and updrafts from the intense head fire. The small amount which reached the ground was immediately evaporated by the intense heat of the fire. After nightfall, in cooler conditions, with a rise in air humidity, and less wind, crews were able to contain the fire on the south western boundary of the Park, along Pechey Road, Throssel Road, and the Great Eastern Highway.

About half the park was burnt out, in a great swathe from the north east to the south west corner. Several houses in the adjoining suburbs of Swanview and Greenmount were destroyed by fires caused by ember showers. The wind change also sent ember showers over Darlington and Glen Forrest, and houses were burnt, due to ignition of coconut fibre doormats, or leaf choked gutters. Two people in Greenmount died, one from a heart attack, and one from asthma caused by smoke inhalation. The Rangers' office and the Tavern were also destroyed.

The news media arrived at the scene in a helicopter at about the time the rangers died. That day attempts were made, without success, to interview the Minister for the Environment and DBCA's Director of National Parks. The state Premier did appear on the evening news, saying what a great tragedy it was, and the government would be taking steps to ensure that it never happened again.

The ferocity of the fire killed large trees in the park, which would take centuries to replace. Many native animals, including possums and kangaroos died. Some smaller animals died in the scorching flare of long unburnt *balga* thatches, and the kangaroos were killed because, due to long fire exclusion, the scrub was thick, and hampered their escape.

The following spring, however, most *balga* in the burnt area flowered, as did many orchids which had not been seen for years, being smothered under the heavy litter. There were spectacular flowerings of *Hovea*, *Lechenaultia*, and *Kennedya*. The *djiridji* (zamias) in the burnt area put up new shoots within a few weeks of the fire, and over the next two years flourished and produced bright red fruit (*byoo*), as they had when *Noongars* deliberately burnt them, long before.

Within a week of the fire, the remaining kangaroos, avid for nitrogen, were seen feeding on the tiny green shoots in the burnt area, and on the juicy young leaves at the heart of the shorter grass trees. They had been unable to reach these for years, due to the thick barrier of unburnt thatch. Due to increased nutrient supply following the fire, in the following winter they produced a number of joeys, which more than replaced the adults killed in the fire.

About four or five years after the fire, litter fuel had again built up, locking up scarce nutrients. The orchids and trigger plants began to disappear, and the *djiridji* leaves also began to turn yellow, starting with the mid rib. The leaves of most plants became harder, and smaller, and a drab shade of green, due to lack of nutrients, particularly nitrogen. Seed production was poor, and many were, in fact, only empty husks, without endosperm. Unfortunately, there were no *Noongars*, who had empathy for such changes in the plants, to revive them again with light summer fires, in what they called '*narik*', or land ready to be burnt again. Tonnes of leaves, sticks, and seed capsules continued to build up, until the next serious fire occurred, about twenty years later, from a lightning strike.

After the fire of 2051, local residents began to question the wisdom of having a National Park next to suburban dwellings. Although real conservation was, quite rightly, still a major concern in informed quarters, some local councillors and real estate agents began successfully to urge that the land be released for housing blocks. A 'nature' estate of 5 to 20 hectare blocks was established, albeit choked with dense thickets of Parrot Bush due to the last fierce fire. Some spectacular homes were built amongst the native vegetation along Jane Brook and its tributaries. A network of horse trails was laid out. Each owner was required to sign a covenant protecting the native plants and animals. Unfortunately, native vegetation and housing, especially houses with timber decking, do not have a long term prospect in a fire prone environment. A fierce fire in the 2060s destroyed some of the houses, with some loss of human life. Most survivors quietly sold their houses as soon as possible, and prices fell.

After this fire, politicians debated the future of the area. One proposition was to convert the National Park into a camp for floods of desperate economic refugees from the Middle East, Africa and parts of Asia, where water and food supplies had run out, and fighting had been rampant for decades. Another was to invite private investors to convert the park into a profit making enterprise, with a casino and heliport, so relieving the public purse of further expense.

-oOo-

Essay 20

Thank You Rudyard, Thomas and Robert

I keep six honest serving-men
(They taught me all I knew)
Their names are What and Why and When
And How and Where and Who.'

Rudyard Kipling, Just So Stories, 1902

Rudyard Kipling was a talented writer, but I suspect that, like most writers, he also read a great deal. Before writing the 'Just So Stories', he possibly read a sentence written by Thomas Wilson over four hundred years earlier, in the reign of Queen Elizabeth the First.

Tom Wilson was a scholar at Cambridge University, with particular interests in logic and rhetoric. Although not well-known today, he was associated with Lord Burleigh, Queen Elizabeth's High Treasurer, who funded her Secret Service. This service was run by her State Secretary, Sir Francis Walsingham.

Tom Wilson's original sentence was *'Who, What and Where, by What Help, Why, How, When, doe many things disclose.'*, which sounds like good advice for a spymaster. Both Rudyard and Tom have given us a memorable key to creating systematic question-maps of the truth in any complex human situation.

Going even further back in history, Aristotle is also credited with systematically seeking truth by means of the syllogism (Essay 15), a form of deductive reasoning, with two premises, and a conclusion drawn from them. An old example, I'm sure still offered in philosophy classes at Oxford and Cambridge, is:

Major Premise: All humans eventually die.
Minor Premise: Socrates is human.
Conclusion: Therefore Socrates will eventually die.

Aristotle, like Tom Wilson, dabbled in logic and rhetoric, and noticed the problem of illicit syllogisms, with either false premises, or some missing. Such illicit syllogisms could be accidental, but were sometimes deliberately used for deception, notably in the rhetoric of political meetings and law courts. He called illicit syllogisms, whether deliberate or not, '*enthymemes*'. Another term, with similar meaning to '*enthymeme*', and similar origin to '*syllogism*', is '*paralogism*'. In modern English this last word is mainly used to describe false reasoning which is not deliberate, but simply due to insufficient thinking. That is the sense in which I will use it, both here and elsewhere (Essay 21).

Both kinds of illicit thinking are still common today, perhaps even more so than formerly. I am sure that we are all guilty of inadvertent paralogisms. Now, not only do enthymemes still appear in law and politics, but also in the news media, social media, advertising, international intelligence bluffing, and even, occasionally, in our revered refereed scientific literature. I am sure that most of those mistakes and omissions appearing in scientific literature are paralogisms, that is to say not deliberate, but by oversight.

Nevertheless, scientific authors and referees could learn much from those judges and lawyers who make us swear to tell the truth, the whole truth, and nothing but the truth. They might even learn from spymasters, who have to peruse potentially deep or misleading documents, or writers who grew up in India, and tried to understand that vast and ancient land, with its bewildering array of people, cultures, languages, and intrigue.

As an historical example, an instance of one or more possible shortfalls in the truth or range of premises, with potentially regrettable effects on understanding, judgement, action and outcome is given below. It is perhaps surprising to find a story of the Vietnam War in a book about Australian bushfire. Yet war and bushfire management do have some similarities. For instance, napalm is a very unpleasant cause of fire, with past dire effects upon the Vietnamese. Had they been acutely aware of those effects, might the architects of that war been less belligerent?

An American Paralogism based on Statistics

Although descriptive statistics, reasoning from general to particular, have long been used by humans, I believe the use of inductive statistics, trying to reason from the particular to the general, began only in the early nineteenth century with the Belgian mathematician Adolphe Quetelet. He studied, amongst other fascinating matters, the probability of cavalry troopers being killed by horse kicks. This analysis was potentially useful in predicting the future need for recruiting drives. He used a relatively small sample of past fatal horse kicks to inductively model the total number of future fatal horse kicks, but I have no idea how useful it was, eventually, to recruiting.

Across the English Channel, it wasn't until the late nineteenth century that Francis Galton, the police detective's friend, peered into the forensic possibilities of finger prints, and the early twentieth century when the rivals Karl Pearson and Sir Ronald Fisher led to a blossoming of inductive statistics as a tool for science generally, and agricultural science in particular. In more recent times inductive statistics have been used in high political and military places, to predict future outcomes of elections and wars. Yet there have been some spectacular failures.

Such an inductive failure involves Robert S. McNamara, who was the United States Secretary for Defense during the Vietnam War. A cautionary tale about his use of statistics has been told by a sharply intelligent historian, the late Barbara Tuchman, in her book *The March of Folly*, a history of wars from biblical times up to Vietnam.

According to Barbara Tuchman, McNamara studied statistics at the Harvard Business School before World War 2. He had an eyesight problem, so during that war he was used to apply statistical methods to plan movements of troops, aircraft, and supplies. He did accurate work, and after World War 2 was rewarded with the presidency of the Ford Motor Company, where his statistical approach to management was again applauded. Regarded as one of the *'brightest and best'*, his next move was into politics, first as Secretary of Defense under President Kennedy, then under President Johnson. McNamara understood the mechanics of statistics, but he seems to have had little understanding of the people, history and politics of Vietnam, nor the uncertainties of military information and combat, once neatly described by the astute General von Clausewitz as the *'fog of war'*.

In 1961 Ngho Diem, then president of South Vietnam, requested that American troops be sent to his country to resist attacks by the Vietcong of North Vietnam. General Maxwell Taylor was sent to investigate the situation, and recommended that such aid be given. However, President Kennedy was initially wary, and suggested that only advisory and technical troops should be sent. Within a year or so, Vietcong attacks increased, so American combat troops were sent.

At first there was optimism that the world's leading superpower would quickly prevail. One optimist was Robert S. McNamara. Despite warning from at least one experienced general, McNamara was very keen to reduce warfare to a statistical *'model'*, using inductive statistics for *'war management'*, so he issued instructions to US field commanders to submit body counts after every action. At an early stage, these were claimed to be 3:5 in favour of the United States and its South Vietnamese ally versus the Vietcong. On this evidence, possibly adding in the tonnage of bombs dropped on North Vietnam, McNamara rhetorically announced that '*Every quantitative measurement we have shows we are winning this war*'. Later, when things were clearly not going in favour of the United States, the Defense Secretary's reasoning was dubbed '*The McNamara Fallacy*' by sociologist Daniel Yankelovitch. This can be found on the Worldwide Web.

A question-map may help to summarize some possible mistakes. For example, who made the body counts, and were they reliable? Were the figures submitted from the field sometimes manipulated, for reasons best known to the commanders who submitted them? Was this an example of the '*fog of war*' mentioned above? Did they include simple village folk, old people, or even children? According to Barbara Tuchman, wounded US soldiers were quickly flown home. If they died there, were they then excluded from body counts for the fighting in Vietnam? Apart from casualties, were matters such as troop morale, training, knowledge of terrain, and history considered?

Most people now know the outcome of the Vietnam War. McNamara, some other politicians, and some American voters, seem to have deceived themselves by an enthymeme, or perhaps, to be kinder, a paralogism.

To be fair to Robert, after that war he published a book openly discussing the errors of judgement. Readers must make up their own minds on the possibility of later paralogisms on wars in Iraq and Afghanistan, and their outcomes.

Yet could there similarly be errors in the use of statistical reasoning in refereed papers on bushfire ecology? We may ask what errors, and why and when they were made, and how, and where, and who made them? Like Tom Wilson and Rudyard Kipling, the philosopher Lord Verulam was much interested in truth, so, in the next essay, he might be able to help us.

-oOo-

Essay 21

Back to Lord Verulam

The enquiry of truth, which is the love-making, or wooing of it, the knowledge of truth, which is the presence of it, and the belief of truth, which is the enjoying of it, is the sovereign good of human nature.'

Francis Bacon, Essay 'Of Truth' (1625)

Remembering the preface at the start of this book, perhaps we can see Francis Bacon's view of truth as involving hindsight, insight, and foresight. Firstly, any question about bushfire can be subjected to historical or archaeological research into past events; then on scientific insight into past, present and future; then an eventual confident belief in a particular view of bushfire truth, on which we can happily base decisions for the future.

In Essay 15, I gave a light hearted example of an illicit syllogism by Ambrose Bierce, whom I am sure intended to amuse rather than deceive. It used correct mathematical logic, but arrived at a false conclusion due to a deliberately false premise. Below I give two examples of refereed, scientific papers, about bushfire, where unintentional paralogisms, overlooked by both authors and referees, may have appeared. Would identifying these possible paralogisms make us happier in our grasp of the truth, so we can better identify future bushfire practice and policy?

Potential paralogisms in burning swamps in south-west Australia

Professor Pierre Horwitz, of West Australia's Edith Cowan University, has published a number of refereed papers which present evidence that burning of peat swamps in south-west Australia can be harmful. Dry peat, when burnt in summer or early autumn, can smoulder for weeks, or even months, destroying large amounts, and chemically altering the remnants. This is a serious ecological matter, and Professor Horwitz and his colleagues should be congratulated for drawing attention to it. Yet did they overlook a few matters? Let's try a question-map.

Might some peat swamp rushes, or sedges such as Semaphor Sedge (*Mesomelaena tetragona*), be capable of burning even when standing in water? Might they have been burnt by *Noongar* people, in their seasons of *makuru* to *djilba* (roughly winter), at times when the peat itself was underwater, and so would not burn? Might *Noongar* people have done this to harvest the edible roots of some rushes and reduce midges or mosquitoes around their camps? Would burning across the water, in appropriate weather, have given the water a beneficial dose of smoke, so germinating many seeds as the water dried later in the year (*djilba* to *kambarang*)? Might winter burning be a better way of managing peat swamps than trying to ban fire from them altogether? Might banning fire altogether from swamps lead to invasion by native or exotic shrubs and trees, and long term drying of the swamps?

I have briefly contacted Professor Horwitz on the matter, but after an equally brief reply, he has chosen not to continue the conversation. I remain open to discussion, as one might expect in science.

The potential paralogism lies, of course, in the assumption that peat swamp fires can, and did only occur in the *Noongar* summer seasons of *kambarang* to *bunuru*, when the peat was dry enough to burn. It would be useful to see if any *Noongar* Elders have views on this. I hope Professor Horwitz will join, or even initiate, any such discussion.

Paralogisms in the Kwongan?

There is a long standing dispute in south-west Australia over the reliability of interpreting thousands of black, horizontal rings discovered by me, under the charcoal layer common on the stems of *balga* grasstrees (*Xanthorrhoea spp.*). These rings can clearly be caused by fire, since deliberate burning of a *balga* produces them. It has been suggested that other causes, such as smoke alone, can cause them. This may be so, but it has yet to be proved, and the research would be challenging, because the most common cause of smoke is, of course, fire. I hope someone will have the time, energy, and financial support to look into this matter. I would be happy to help.

The *balga* technique is similar to the well established one long used in dating past fires in cross sections of old dicotyledonous trees in Europe and the United States, as described by F.C. Craighead (1927). The difference is that *balga* are monocotyledons, so the growth and fire rings occur up the stem, rather than outward from the core. I regard dendrochronology as a branch of archaeology.

More than twenty years ago, after using the *balga* technique on hundreds of *balga* in the *jarrah*, *tuart* and *wandoo* forests, and the *banksia* woodlands just north of Perth, I was invited by a group of academics, led by Dr. Neal Enright, Dr. Ben Miller, and Professor Byron Lamont, to use it in *kwongan* heath near Eneabba. At their request, I examined two sites, Yardanogo Reserve and Beekeeper's Reserve.

A few years earlier, I believe this group of academics had published a statistical *'Dynamic Seedbank Model'*, created for them with help from one or more German statisticians. The model suggested that burning *kwongan* at less than ten year intervals would be harmful to two local native species, *Banksia attenuata* and *Banksia hookeriana*.

Neither of these plants resprouts after death from fire, both relying on winged seeds dispersed from woody cones. The distance to which these winged seeds are dispersed from their parent tree was calculated by Dr. Enright and others, as base data for the mathematical model, by counting seeds in trays set out beneath the trees. They arrived at a statistical maximum dispersal distance of only a few metres. This number was then, presumably, used as a premise in the *Dynamic Seedbank Model*.

It is not clear to me whether the academics, in their model, took account of several other potential premises, such as that winged *Banksia* seeds are almost certainly dispersed for much further than a few metres by cockatoos, and also by small whirlwinds called *willie-willies*, which commonly occur near Eneabba on both recently burnt areas, and probably also on areas of the black ilmenite sand which is mined in the area. This information on cockatoos and *willie-willies* was given to them, as far as I remember, by the then Eneabba caravan park manager, a keen naturalist.

Use of the statistical model then concluded that fires at intervals less than a decade would reduce the seed bank, and so lead to eventual local extinction of the two *Banksia* plants. Given the widespread presence of *balga* at Eneabba, the academics presumably hoped that the *balga* technique would confirm their statistical model.

It did not. At the Yardanogo Reserve, it showed that fire intervals back in the nineteenth century had been commonly less than ten years. The Enright group then concluded, and claimed in the scientific literature, that the *balga* technique was not only '*unreliable*' at Eneabba, but everywhere else in south-west Australia.

Fifteen *balga* were examined at Yardanogo. For readers' interest, the fire dates on three of the oldest *balga* from Yardanogo Reserve are shown below. These were observed in 1999. The reserve is in sandy dunes, so one *balga* was selected from the moist swale, one from the midslope, and one from the dry ridge.

113

Balga No. 15 (swale) Fires at 1888, 1890, 1892, 1894, 1897, 1901, 1905, 1911, 1915, 1918, 1920, 1924, 1928, 1935, 1944, 1946, 1952, 1954, 1956, 1964, 1967, 1985, then unburnt up to, and including, 1999.

Balga No. 2 (midslope) Fires at 1874, 1878, 1883, 1888, 1894, 1897, 1902, 1909, 1914, 1921, 1925, 1932, 1935, 1951, 1959, 1966, 1979, 1984, 1991, then unburnt up to, and including, 1999.

Balga No. 10 (ridge) Fires at 1859, 1862, 1866, 1868, 1870, 1874, 1879, 1882, 1889, 1898, 1900, 1904, 1909, 1919, 1926, 1934, 1944, 1966, 1981, then unburnt up to, and including, 1999.

It will be seen that frequent fire intervals of less than ten years occurred in the nineteenth, and early twentieth century. In my opinion, they call into question the reliability of the '*Dynamic Seedbank Model*'. It will be recalled (Essay 14) that a newspaper correspondent called '*Sandy Farmer*' described biennial, therefore patchy fire, east of the Darling Scarp, in 1845. He thought it did the sandy country vegetation good. I can see no reason for him to lie, or be mistaken in his observations.

Obviously unhappy with the above *balga* results, the academics then invited me to examine further *balga* in Beekeeeeper's Reserve, just south-west of Yardanogo Reserve. The *balga* there were generally much shorter, younger, and contorted, than those at Yardanogo, or in earlier sampling in forests further south. The contortions are probably due to frequent past flowering caused by frequent fire, and they sometimes made accurate dating difficult.

The Enright group asked me to provide them with Beekeeper Reserve fire dates on *balga*, which Dr. Miller then compared with some satellite fire data for the period 1973-2002. In comparison, the oldest *balga* at the Beekeeper site went back to the 1920s. However, as at Yardanogo Reserve, the *balga* showed more frequent fire before satellite data were available. We should note that at least one paper in the refereed literature (Price *et al.*), from the Northern Territory, states that satellite data there were found unreliable for patchily burnt areas, since they could not identify unburnt patches less than ten metres across.

For brevity, as at Yardanogo, only three of the oldest *balga* for Beekeeper's Reserve are given below. This reserve is much flatter than Yardanogo Reserve, so the terms swale, midslope and ridge are not used. It will be seen that the *balga* again contradict the idea that the reserve was historically burnt at only greater than ten year intervals.

114

Balga No. 7 Fires at 1922, 1926, 1931, 1936, 1940, 1946, 1949, 1955, 1966, 1975, 1992, then unburnt up to, and including, 2004.

Balga No. 42 Fires at 1932, 1934, 1936, 1938, 1940, 1942, 1946, 1955, 1960, 1971, 1982, 1987, 1995, 2000, then unburnt up to, and including, 2004.

Balga No. 53 Fires at 1920, 1926, 1931, 1937, 1940, 1945, 1953, 1958, 1963, 1969, 1979, 1983, 1987, 1993, 1998, then unburnt up to, and including, 2004.

Given such a sharp difference of opinion over the past frequency burning in *kwongan* heath at Eneabba, we should consider the possible presence of illicit arguments on either side. A question-map may help.

Are the satellite data, the *Dynamic Seedbank Model* , and the *balga* data all to be trusted? We should remember that the satellite data only extend over a much shorter period than the *balga* data. As already noted, workers in the Northern Territory have found that satellite images of patchy fire can be unreliable. The *balga* records agree with hundreds of *balga* records from other vegetation types in other parts of the south-west, and agree with some historical records of traditional fire frequency further south.

Should we trust oral evidence from Eneabba, from one local Aboriginal Elder, and a number of local long-term farmers, that there were, some decades ago, many more Aboriginal people in the area; that the *kwongan* heath was burnt patchily more frequently than at ten year intervals, at least up to the 1950s; and that the lack of recent burning is leading to big and destructive fires, formerly unknown?

One farmer remembers the names of two Aboriginal kangaroo shooters called Brockman, father and son, who hunted up to the nineteen fifties, and habitually set fire to patches of an annual native grass (most likely *Austrostipa compressa*) as they went, in order to produce more grass for kangaroos in the following winter. This may be compared with the report from '*Sandy Farmer*', closer to Perth, in Essay 14.

A member of another farming family, present in the Eneabba area from the 1880s, says his early family members reported narrow, zig-zag fires, lit on a south-east, or easterly land breeze, then backing around to self-extinguish on the same day, on a west or south-west sea breeze. This informant also believes, from family information, that more frequent fires kept mistletoe under control, killing it before it could kill the host trees, but allowing it to create fauna refuge hollows. Now many trees in the *kwongan*, infested with mistletoe, are dying.

The land-sea breeze tactic for burning has been mentioned as normal practice by a descendant of former graziers much further south, in *tuart* forest. It ceased when their leases expired in 1960, and the Yalgorup National Park was established. It will be remembered (Essay 6) that the earliest European settlers, around York, Dandalup, Bunbury and Busselton, repeatedly mentioned traditional fire intervals of only a few years.

Should a mega-fire occur at Eneabba, due to fuel unburnt for ten years or more, I can imagine the cockatoos screeching with indignation as they, and the *willie-willies*, do their best to scatter winged *Banksia* seeds again over a landscape blackened from horizon to horizon. What a pity if *Banksia attenuata, Banksia hookeriana* , and other *kwongan* plants, were all driven to extinction by inappropriately long fire exclusion, due to the presence of one or more paralogisms. Clearly, more careful research is needed, before DBCA makes decisions on fire frequency in *kwongan* bush. Might the clinical terms *'false-negative'* and *'false-positive'*, used by Enright *et al.* about the *balga* data, actually apply rather to the twenty years of relatively recent satellite data used by them as a criterion of truth for only a small part of the *balga* data?

At the same time, I should be cautious of errors in my own research, and will be most interested if the Enright group can demonstrate any to me, without use of the possible paralogism that their relatively short twenty years of satellite data are absolutely reliable.

I hope Lord Verulam can help us, through essays, and question-maps, to sort out a few other tangles in current refereed bushfire literature, so arriving at some sovereign truths, so important to human happiness and progress. Together with sound natural science, I see a vital role in this for fire knowledge drawn from Dreaming Trails. Only *Noongar* people can legitimately help us with this.

-oOo-

Bibliography

The following list of sources (including books, peer-reviewed articles, newspaper reports and other material) will give some idea of the rich extent of bushfire history and science in south-west Australia and elsewhere. It is not a complete reference list on the subject, but will make a good starting point for most readers.

Those who thirst for more may find it within some of these references, or in the bibliography of my thesis, by searching online for (ward+wungong+fire). The notes in italics after some sources may be useful.

A York Settler (1850) Letter to the Editor of The Inquirer, Perth. (*From an angry early European settler, complaining about Noongar burning.*)

Abbott, I. and Burrows, N.B. (2003) Fire in ecosystems of south-west Western Australia: impacts and management. Backhuys, Leiden. (*A mixed bag of useful and not so useful chapters. The best is the careful historical work by the distinguished ecologist, Dr. Ian Abbott.*)

Adams, A.B. (1947) In Search of a Pasture. Article in The Western Mail, Perth, Western Australia, Thursday 9th January. (*Describes the experiences of an early settler at Denmark, on the south coast of south-west Australia. Mentions presence then of Kangaroo Grass, which needs frequent burning to survive long term.*)

Adams, C.C. (1994) The Knot Book. W.H. Freeman and Company, New York. (*An interesting book on mathematical Knot Theory, relevant to Essay18.*)

Aristotle (2012) The Art of Rhetoric. Collins Classics, London. (*Discusses the use of enthymemes in rhetoric.*)

Booysen, Peter de V. & Tainton, Neil M. (1984) Ecological effects of fire in South African ecosystems. Springer-Verlag, Berlin. (*Mention, by two competent scientists, of frequent historical burning in South Africa.*)

Bradshaw, S.D. and Bradshaw, F.J. (2003) Short-term movements and habitat use by the marsupial honey possum *Tarsipes rostratus*. Journal of Zoology, London. **258**: 343-348.

Brockway, G.E. (1923) Fire control organisation and fire fighting operations in Mundaring District. Conference of Western Australian foresters. Australian Forestry Journal. (*Mentions common practice, up to 1920s, of beating out fires with green branches.*)

Burrows, N.B. (2005) Burning Rocks. Article in Landscope 20(4):54, Department of Conservation and Land Management, Perth. (*Describes a major fire in Monadnocks Conservation Park in 2003, caused by lightning, but its ferocity due to lack of regular, pre-emptive burning.*)

Burrows, N. and Middleton, T. (2016) Mechanisms enabling a fire sensitive plant to survive frequent fires in south-west Australian eucalypt forests. Fire Ecology, Vol. 12, Issue 1. (*Without mentioning the balga technique, explains how fire sensitive plants can survive under frequent, therefore light and patchy, burning.*)

Burton Jackson, J.L. (1993) Frowning Fortunes, Hesperian Press, Perth. (*Mention of former abundance of native grasses.*)

Bushfire Control Policy Criticised (1950) Article in West Australian Newspaper, 29 June. (*Complaint by beekeepers that the Forests Department was not burning often enough.*)

Carrell, S. (2008) Survival fight for eagle and hen harrier. Newspaper article, The Guardian, United Kingdom, 22nd April 2008.

Chatwin, B. (1987) The Songlines. Jonathon Cape, London. (*Mentions the use by Aboriginal folk of pathways, songs, dancing, art, and music to remember encyclopaedic information about their country.*)

Colangelo, W.I., Lamont, B.B., Jones, A.S., Ward, D.J. & Bombardieri, S. (2002) The anatomy and chemistry of the colour bands of grasstree stems (*Xanthorrhoea preissii*) as a basis for plant age and fire history determination. Annals of Botany **89**, 605-611. (*Supports the validity of the balga technique.*)

Countryside Alliance (2008) New study links loss of gamekeepers and grouse to declines in waders and hen harriers. www.countryside-alliance.org.uk/moorlands. (*Argument from the UK that when grouse numbers decline, so do waders and hen harriers.*)

Craighead, F. C. (1927) Abnormalities in annual rings resulting from fires. Journal of Forestry 25:840-842. (*Early work on use of trees in America to reconstruct fire history.*)

Darwin, Charles (1859) On the Origin of Species by Means of Natural Selection. Reprint by The Folio Society, London 2006.

De Lange, J.H. and Boucher, C. (1990) Autecological studies on *Audonia capitata* (*Bruniaceae*). Plant-derived smoke as a germination cue. South African Journal of Botany 59: 188-202. (*Original work on effect of smoke on seed germination.*)

Dixon, K.W., Roche, S. and Pate, J. (1995) The promotive effect of smoke derived from burnt native vegetation on seed germination of Western Australian plants. Oecologia 101:185-192. (*Imitative research work in Western Australia five years after the South African work by De Lange and Boucher (1990).*)

De Chardin, Pierre Teilhard (1959) The Phenomenon of Man. Harper Perennial. (*Book by Jesuit archaeologist about the relationship between the natural world and that created by humans. Might be called 'Human Ecology'.*)

Duncan, P. (1981) Seasonal changes in a population of the nectar-feeding marsupial *Tarsipes spencerae* (*Marsupialia: Tarsipedidae*). Journal of Zoology, London. **195**: 267-279.

Drummond, J. (1842-1847) Letters to Sir William Hooker at Kew Herbarium, originals at Kew, copies at WA Herbarium, Perth. (*Found by Dr Lachie McCaw. Drummond advised the use of ash and pruning at intervals of a few years to benefit West Australian plants at Kew. It would be interesting to find out if they still follow this advice. Professor Stephen Hopper, now at the University of Western Australia was director there for a while. Hopper is also a member of the Leeuwin Group (see website), who seem opposed to the regular burning reported by James Drummond.*)

Duhem, P.M.M. (1954) The Aim and Structure of Physical Theory. Princeton University Press. Translated from the original (1906) French by P. Wiener.

Dunning, Luke T., Liabot, Anne-Lise, Olofsson, Jill K., Smith, Emma K., Vorontsova, Maria S., Besnard, Guillaume, Simpson, Kimberley J., Lundgren, Marjorie R., Addicot, Eda, Gallagher, Rachel, V., Yingying, Chu, Pennington, R. Toby, Christin, Pascal-Antoine and Lehman, Caroline, E.R. (2017) The recent and rapid spread of *Themeda triandra*, Botany Letters, Vol 164, No.4, 327-337. (*Many authors – how much did each contribute?*)

Eades, A. (1999) Benefits of Traditional Burning. Letter from then Chairperson of South West Commission of Elders to the Minister for the Environment, Perth. Should be in the Ministerial records. (*Statement by Noongar Elder that jarrah forest was traditionally burned at 3-4 year intervals, and benefited from such short term burning.*)

Enright, N. J., Lamont B. B., and Miller, B. P. (2005) Anomalies in grasstree fire history reconstructions for south-western Australian vegetation. Austral Ecology **30**: 668-673. (*One of the papers published by Enright et al. suggesting the balga technique is 'unreliable' for all south-western vegetation. See Essay 21.*)

Esplin, B., Gill, A.M. and Enright, N. (2003) Report of the Inquiry into the 2002-2003 Victoria Bushfires. Victorian Government, Melbourne. (*Contributed little to bushfire understanding and management in Australia. Criticised by eminent QC.*)

Everaardt, A. (2005) The impact of fire on the endemic Honey Possum. Western Wildlife, **9**(1). Department of CALM, Perth.

Foley, J.C. (1947) A Study of Meteorological Conditions associated with Bush & Grass Fires & Fire Protection Strategy in Australia. Bulletin No. 38, Commonwealth of Australia. (*Detailed list of bushfires in Western Australia back to the nineteenth century.*)

Fox , B.J. and McKay, G.M. (**1981**) Small mammal responses to pyric successional changes in eucalypt forest. Australian Journal of Ecology **6**(1): 29

Friend, G. and Wayne, A. (2003) Relationships between mammals and fire in south-west Western Australan ecosystems. Chapter in Abbott and Burrows (2003), p. 363.

Gammage, Bill (**2011**) The Biggest Estate on Earth: How Aborigines made Australia. Allen & Unwin. (*Well-known book on how Aboriginal fires helped to shape the Australian landscape.*)

Gillibrand, M. (2004) Response to the Review of the Heather and Grass (Burning) Regulations 1986 and the Heather and Grass Burning Code 1994 in England. The Moorland Association, United Kingdom.

Gillison, A.N. (1993) Grasslands of the South Pacific. In Ecosystems of the World, ed. D.W. Goodall, Elsevier, Amsterdam.

Gott, B. (1999) Fire as an Aboriginal management tool in south-eastern Australia. Proceedings of the Australian Bushfire Conference, Albury, Victoria. (*Work by an intelligent botanist on relationship between fire, plants, and Aboriginal people.*)

Goforth, B.R. and Minnich, R.A. (2007) Evidence, exaggeration, and error in historical accounts of chaparral wildfires in California. Ecological Applications **17**(3): 779-790. (*Some good question mapping about paralogisms in California.*)

Gowers, Sir E. (1973) The Complete Plain Words. HM Stationery Office, London. (*Criticised poor use of English in ecology publications.*)

Green, N. (1979) Nyungar – the people. Creative Research, Perth. (*Describes Noongar hunting techniques.*)

Grove TS, O'Connell AM & Malajcuk N (1980) Effects of fire on the growth, nutrient content and rate of nitrogen fixation of the cycad *Macrozamia riedlii*. Australian Journal of Botany **28**: 271-81. (*Notes copious nitrogen fixation for a few years only after fire.*)

Gusfield, J.R. (1981) The Culture of Public Problems. University of Chicago Press. (*Uses concept of 'theatre' to show how 'scientific' findings are not always as neutral as they might be, and how such findings can be simplified by news media, politicians, salesmen etc. to give an 'illusion of certainty, clarity, facticity and authority.' Good quote 'Art and rhetoric have not been sent into perpetual exile to live outside the walls of Science and Knowledge. With or without passport, they steal back into the havens of clinical and antiseptic scholarship and operate from underground stations to lead forays into the headquarters of the enemy.' Also mentions rhetorical use of synecdoche, and root metaphors (Pepper 1966, Black 1962), and 'tacit presuppositions of science' (Polanyi 1962).*)

Hallam, S.J. **(1975)** Fire & Hearth: A Study of Aboriginal Usage and European Usurpation in South-western Australia. Australian Institute of Aboriginal Studies, Canberra. (*Well-known and reliable book by an anthropologist, on Noongar use of fire.*)

Hallam, S.J. **(2002)** Peopled Landscapes in Southwestern Australia in the Early 1800s: Aboriginal Burning Off in the Light of Western Australian Historical Documents. Journal of the Royal Western Australian Historical Society, Perth. (*As above.*)

Harris, J. (1835) Article in Perth Gazette, February 21st. 'Expedition to the Hotham.' (*Description of lush grass along the route by Dr J. Harris, father of J. S. Harris below.*)

Harris, J.S. (1882) Comments in Fraser (1882) General Information Respecting the Present Condition of the Forests and Timber Trade of the Southern Part of the Colony. Government Printer, Perth, Western Australia. (*Harris grew up in south-west Australia, had close contact with Noongar people, and recommended frequent burning of the eucalypt forest.*)

Harris, A.C. and Wallace, W.R. (1959) Controlled Burning in Western Australian Forest Practice. Typescript in former Forests Dept. (now DBCA) library, Como, Western Australia.

Hassell, E. **(1936)** Notes on the ethnology of the Wheelman Tribe of Southwestern Australia. Anthropos 31:679-711. (*Mentions widespread and regular use of fire by Noongar people near the south coast of Western Australia, preceded by a dance. Mentions great importance of women in burning, and copious smoke. Care taken to conserve young birds.*)

Heather Trust (2007) Launch of the Heather and Grass Burning Code 2007 for England. http://www.heathertrust.co.uk/heatherburning/.

Hudson, P.J., Newborn, D. and Dobson, A.P. (1992) Regulation and stability of a free-living host-parasite system, *Trichostrongylus tenuis* in Red Grouse. Monitoring and parasite reduction experiments. Journal of Animal Ecology **61**: 477-486. (*Examines the benefits of regular burning of heather in reducing ticks and their viruses.*)

Hudson, P.J., Norman, R. and Laurensen, M.K. (1995) Persistence in tick-borne viruses: *Ixodes ricinus* and louping ill in Red Grouse. Parasitology **111**: 49-58.

Hudson, P.J. and Newborn, D. (1995) A Manual of Red Grouse and Moorland Management. The Game Conservancy Trust, Fordingbridge, Hampshire.

Horwitz, P., Judd, S. and Sommer, B. (2003) Fire and organic substrates: soil structure, water quality and biodiversity in far south-west Western Australia. Chapter in Abbott and Burrows (2003). *(Chapter claims, probably correctly, that burning organically rich soil in dry weather is harmful. However, the authors seem unaware of the possibility that Noongar people burnt such areas over standing water, in winter, so conserving the organic matter. There is a need for reliable research by scientists, historians and anthropologists into this matter.)*

Hume, D. (1748) An Enquiry Concerning Human Understanding. Oxford University Press 1999. *(Well-known old philosophy book.)*

Hutchins, D.E. (1916) A Discussion of Australian Forestry: With Special Reference to Forestry in Western Australia. Government Printer, Perth, Western Australia. *(Report by visiting British forest expert who disliked fire, yet mentions traditional frequent burning by Noongars at 3-4 year intervals.)*

Jackson, R.H. and Castillo, E. (1995) Indians, Franciscans, and Spanish Colonization: The Impact of the Mission System on California Indians. The University of New Mexico Press. *(Some history of the Chumash people of California.)*

Keeley, J.E. and Fotheringham, C.J. (2001) Historic fire regime in Southern California shrublands. Conservation Biology **15**: 1536-1548. *(See Minnich et al. for counter arguments.)*

Keeley, J.E. and Zedler, P.H. (2009) Large, high intensity fire events in southern California shrublands: debunking the fine-grain age patch model. Ecological Applications **19**(1): 69-94. *(As above.)*

Kappraff, J. (1991) Connections: The Geometric Bridge between Art and Science. McGraw-Hill Inc. *(Relevant to the unwise government proposal of the acronym STEM as a guide for education in Australia.)*

Kelly, G. (2000) *Karla Wongi*: A Nyungar perspective on forest burning. Special Fire Edition, Landscope Magazine, Department of CALM, Perth, Western Australia. *(Informative article by a Noongar man on fire near the south-west coast of Australia.)*

Kelly, L. (2016) The Memory Code. Allen and Unwin, Crows Nest, NSW, Australia. *(Book on songlines in places other than Australia.)*

Kozlowski, T.T. and Ahlgren, C.E. (1974) Fire and Ecosystems. Academic Press, New York. *(Discussion on the chemical and bacterial effects of fire on soil.)*

Kull, C.A. (2002a) Madagascar's burning issue: the persistent conflict over fire. Environment **44**(3):8-19.

Kull, C.A. (2002b) Madagascar aflame: landscape burning as peasant protest, resistance, or a resource management tool? Political Geography **21**(7): 927-53.

Kull, C. A. (2006) Isle of Fire: The Political Ecology of Landscape Burning in Madagascar. University of Chicago Press *(Madagascar was ruled by the French for about 100 years, but attempts at official abolition of traditional burning by the Malagasy people failed. It was difficult to police – fires were usually unattended, because local people knew where they would stop. The French blamed fire for deforestation, desertification, soil degradation and erosion. Fire was used by the Malagasy to stimulate grass, clear thick bush, and deter locusts and ticks – a key human management tool.)*

Lane-Poole, C.E. (1921) Forests Department Annual Report to Parliament. Government Printer, Perth, Western Australia. *(First Western Australian Conservator of Forests, advised by Hutchins, who disliked fire for what he saw as adverse effects on timber yield.)*

Liacos, L.G. (1973) Present Studies and History of Burning in Greece, Proceedings of Tall Timbers Fire Ecology Conference, Tallahassee, Florida. *(Greek shepherds burnt shrubs to refresh grazing for goats.)*

Loehle, C. (2004) Applying landscape principles to fire hazard reduction. Forest Ecology and Management **198**: 261-267. *(Competent mathematical model which supports deliberate, patchy burning of a proportion of the landscape to avoid big, uncontrollable fires.)*

Lovat, Lord. (1911) The Grouse in Health and Disease. Smith, Elder and Co., London. *(Information from a former prominent land owner in Scotland.)*

Lunt, I.D. (1995) Seed longevity of six native forbs in a closed *Themeda triandra* grassland. Aust. J. Botany, 43,439-449. *(Need for frequent, regular burning of Kangaroo Grass to maintain it.)*

Mbow, C., Nielsen, T.T., and Rasmussen, K. (2000) Savanna fires in east-central Senegal: Distribution patterns, resource management and perceptions. Human Ecology 28(4): 561-583. *(Authors recommend that the Government of Senegal adopt the traditional grass burning habits of local graziers.)*

McCaw, L. and Hanstrum, B. (2003) Fire environment of Mediterranean south-west Western Australia. Chapter in Burrows and Abbott (2003), p.87.

McGillivray, J. (1996) An Economic Study of Grouse Moors. Game Conservancy Scottish Research Trust.

McNamara, R.S. and VanDeMark, B. (1995) In retrospect: The tragedy and lessons of Vietnam. Random House. *(Robert McNamara admits errors in USA policy during the Vietnam War.)*

Miller, G.R. and Watson, A. (1973) Some effects of fire in the Scottish highlands. Proceedings of Tall Timbers Fire Ecology Conference No. 13, Tallahassee, Florida.

Minnich, R. A. (2001) An integrated model of two fire regimes. Conservation Biology, **15**(6)

Mitchell, T.L. (1848) Journal of an expedition into the interior of tropical Australia in search of a route from Sydney to the Gulf of Carpentaria. Longman, London. (*Major Mitchell was one of the first Europeans to note the ecological web of fire, grass, kangaroos and humans.*)

Mulvaney, J. & Green, N. (1992) Commandant of Solitude: The Journals of Captain Collet Barker 1828-1831. Melbourne University Press. (*Captain Collet Barker was an intelligent, thoughtful man, with very bad handwriting, painstakingly translated by the authors, hence the late publication.*)

Nannup, N. (1996) Dreaming Trails Map. DBCA library, Perth, Western Australia. (*Map, by a well-known Noongar Elder, of Dreaming Trails, also known as songlines, or bidi-bidi, for south-west Australia.*)

Naveh, Z. (1973) The ecology of fire in Israel. Proceedings of Tall Timbers Fire Ecology Conference No. 13, Tallahassee, Florida.

Naveh, Z. and Lieberman, A. (1994) Landscape Ecology: Theory and Application, Second Edition. Springer-Verlag, New York.

Neale, M. & Kelly, L. (2020) Songlines: The Power and the Promise, First Knowledges Series, Thames and Hudson, Australia. (*Very interesting book on the use of songlines to maintain traditional Aboriginal knowledge.*)

One Who Has Seen (1950) Letter to Editor of The Daily News, Perth, 5 April. (*Suggests that fire managers and fighters should learn from Aboriginal traditional burning.*)

Parkington, J. (1977) Soaqua: Hunter-fisher-gatherers of the Olifant's River Valley, Western Cape. African Studies 31: 221-343. (*Distinguished South African scholar, who gives intriguing information on past fire in South Africa. In Booysen and Tainton 1984).*

Philips, R., Tomlinson, S., Jennings, S., Holley, B. (2004) The summer ecophysiology of the honey possum (*Tarsipes rostratus*) on the south coast of Western Australia. Honours projects, University of Western Australia.

Picozzi, N. (1968) Grouse bags in relation to the management and geology of heather moors. Journal of Applied Ecology **5**:483-488. (*Concluded that numbers of grouse were maximised by burning many small fires on a 10-12 year rotation. Best result was with about 6 fires crossed per kilometre, and each fire no more than about a hectare.*)

Polanyi, M. (1962) Personal Knowledge. University of Chicago Press. (*Tacit presuppositions of science.*)

Posamentier, H. and Recher, H.F. (1974) The status of *Pseudomys novaehollandiae* (the New Holland Mouse). Australian Journal of Zoology **18**: 66-71. (*Similarities to Honey Possum's relationship to fire.*)

Price, O., Russell-Smith, J., and Edwards, A. (2003) Fine-scale patchiness of different fire intensities in sandstone heath vegetation in northern Australia. International Journal of Wildland Fire, **12**, 227-236. (*Points out that satellite images are, at least in the Northern Territory, unreliable in distinguishing unburnt patches less than ten metres across, within large burnt areas. Might satellite images also be unreliable for small burnt patches in large unburnt areas, in West Australian kwongan heath?*)

Pyne, S.J. (1982) Fire in America: A Cultural History of Wildland and Rural Fire. Princeton University Press. (*Interesting account of traditional burning in America.*)

Pyne, S.J. (1991) Burning Bush: A Fire History of Australia. Henry Holt & Company, New York. (*Very informative on bushfire in Australia, by the world's best fire historian.*)

Pyne, S.J. (2003) Fire's Lucky Country. Introduction to Abbott and Burrows 2003.

Quine, W. Van O. (1953) Two Dogmas of Empiricism, in From a Logical Point of View, Harvard University Press. (*Quine adapted Duhem's physics into philosophy.*)

Rackham, O. (2003) Fire in the European Mediterranean. Aridlands Newsletter No. 54.

Ribet, N. (1998) Essay in *Brûlages dirigé. Pastum No. 51-52, Bulletin de l'Association française de pastoralism –Réseau des équipes de brûlage dirigé. Editions Mimosa, Pérois.*

Richardson, K.C. and Wooller, R.D. (1991) The effect of fire on honey possum populations. Report to World Wide Fund for Nature, Australia.

Russell, E.M. (1986) Observations on the behaviour of the honey possum (*T. rostratus*) in captivity. Australian Journal of Zoology (Supplement) **121**:1-63.

Sandy Farmer (1845) Letter to the Inquirer, Perth, Wednesday 29 January. (*Mentions two year burning by Noongar people on sandy country east of the Darling Range in the 1840s. Was this kwongan?*)

Sand-Jensen, K. (2007) How to write consistently boring scientific literature. Oikos 116(5):723-727. (*A funny essay on the bumbling nature of some scientific papers.*)

Smith, Alexander McCall (2004) The Two and a Half Pillars of Wisdom. Little, Brown Book Club, London. (*A combination of three novels about the celebrated Professor Dr. Moritz-Maria von Igelveld and his academic colleagues at the Institute of Romance Philology, who write many papers and attend many conferences.*)

St. John, Henry, 1st Earl of Bolingbroke (1752) Letters on the Study and Use of History. The Oxford Dictionary of Quotations (1996), Oxford University Press.

Stoate, T.N. and Helms, A.D. (1938) Stocktaking in the jarrah bush 1928-38. Typescript Forests Department (now DBCA), Perth, Western Australia. (*Information on the jarrah forest in the 1930s. Common frequency of fire then 3-4 years.*)

Stokes, John Lort (1840) Voyage of HMS Beagle 1837-1843, Vol. II, Ch. 2.6. (*By courtesy of Gutenberg Press*). (*Stokes saw Noongar people burning the bush just north of Albany, in November, and was impressed by their skill.*)

Stretton, L.E.B. (1938) Report of the Royal Commission to Inquire into the Bushfires of January 1939. Government Printer, Melbourne. (*A practical, perceptive report, unlike some more recent ones.*)

Swift, J. (1726) Gulliver's Travels, Motte, London. (*Ridules some politics.*)

Timbrook, J. (2007) Chumash Ethnobotany: Plant Knowledge among the Chumash People of Southern California. Santa Barbara Museum of Natural History Monographs. (*Most interesting and relevant work on traditional ethnobotany, including mention of fire.*)

Tuchman, Barbara W. (1984) The March of Folly. The Folio Society, London. (*A history of wars from biblical times up to Vietnam in the 1960s. Includes discussion of the perils of false reasoning by Robert McNamara.*)

Vancouver, G. (1798) A Voyage of Discovery to the North Pacific Ocean and round the World in the Years 1790-1795 in the Discovery Sloop of War and Armed Tender Chatham, under the Command of Captain George Vancouver, London. In First Impressions of Albany: Travellers' Tales 1791-1901. Compiled & Published by Sellick, 1997. (*Vancouver noted widespread use of fire by Aboriginal people on the south coast of Western Australia.*)

Von Clausewitz, C. (1989). On War. Translation by Michael Howard and Peter Paret. Everyman's Library, Random House. (*Original version, in German, was published by the author's wife in 1832. There is some debate on the accuracy of various translations.*)

Wallace, W.R. (1965) Fire in the jarrah forest environment. Journal of the Royal Society of Western Australia, Vol. 49, Part 2, p.33-44. (*Wallace was a Conservator of Forests, knowledgeable about bushfire.*)

Ward, D. (1996) Reconstructing pre-European fire history in south-west Australian forests. Proceedings of 13th. International Conference on Fire & Forest Meteorology, Lorne, Australia. (*The earliest, sketchy account of the balga technique.*)

Ward, D. and Van Didden, G. (1997) Reconstructing the fire history of the *jarrah* forest of south-western Australia, a report to Environment Australia, Canberra, from former Dept. of CALM, Perth. (*Uses a large sample of balga stems to show traditional burning of 3-4 year intervals at many places in the jarrah forest.*)

Ward, D. (1998) Fire, Flogging, Measles & Grass: Nineteenth Century Land Use. Essay in DBCA library, Perth, Western Australia. (*Mentions legal steps taken by an early Governor to attempt suppression of regular burning by Noongars. Attempt was only partially successful.*)

Ward, D. & Sneeuwjagt, R. (1999) Believing the Balga: A Time Capsule of Fire History. Autumn Issue, Landscope Magazine, DBCA library, Perth, Western Australia. (*A straightforward magazine account of the balga technique of reconstructing fire history. Rick Sneeuwjagt is an experienced bushfire manager.*)

Ward, D. (2000) Trouble in the Tuart. Report on Yalgorup National Park in DBCA library, Perth, Western Australia. (*The use of the balga technique in the tuart forest of Yalgorup National Park. Also mentions burning practice by settlers there from 1860 to 1960, using breeze change from land to sea. Probably learnt from Noongars.*)

Ward, D. (2001) The Past and Future of Fire in John Forest National Park. Report in DBCA library, Perth, Western Australia. (*The use of the balga technique in John Forrest National Park. It found frequent burning (2-4 year intervals) back at least to the 1840s.*)

Ward, D., Lamont, B. & Burrows, C. (2001) Grasstrees reveal contrasting fire regimes in eucalypt forest before and after European settlement of southwestern Australia. Forest Ecology & Management 150:323-329. (*Lamont's name appeared on several early papers on the balga work, sometimes placing himself as lead author, but later rejoined his colleague Enright in attacking the balga work, presumably in defence of their former joint work on the Dynamic Seedbank Model for kwongan.*)

Ward, D. and Van Didden, G. (2003) A Brief Fire History of Monadnocks Conservation Park, Western Australia. Report to the Department of Conservation and Land Management, Perth, Western Australia. (*The use of the balga technique after a fierce bushfire in Monadnocks Conservation Park showed regular frequent burning (2-4 years) up to the 1930s.*)

Ward, D. (2010) People, Fire and Water in Wungong Catchment. Open access online PhD thesis, Curtin University. (ward+wungong+fire) (*Description of the balga technique with historical and geographical background, and chemical and colour research into old fire marks. Also discusses the kwongan dispute.*)

Weins, D., Renfree, M. and Wooller, R.D. (1979) Pollen loads of honey possums (*Tarsipes spencerae*) and non-flying mammal pollination in south-western Australia. Annals of the Missouri Botanical Gardens. **66**: 830-838.

Welsh, D.J.A. **(1993)** Complexity: Knots, Colourings and Countings. London Mathematical Society Lecture Note Series 186. Cambridge University Press. (*Knot Theory referred to in Essay 18.*)

West, O. **(1971)** Fire, man and wildlife as interacting factors limiting the development of climax vegetation in Rhodesia. Proceedings of the Tall Timbers Fire Ecology Conference No. 11, Tallahassee, Florida. (*Oliver West was an astute human ecologist, whether he used that title or not. He raised the question of long use of fire for honey gathering by Africans, which involved long co-operation between humans and the Honey Guide bird. Also discussed fire as a hunting tool in Africa, both to promote grass, and to drive animals. In the Ndebele tribe, only chiefs were allowed to use fire for hunting. For the benefit of cattle, the area around the Ndebele King's Kraal at Bulawayo was burnt in three large segments, one each year in the dry season, so a three year cycle. Interesting note of the belief amongst Africans that burning is needed to ensure a good rainy season – do Aboriginal people have similar ideas? Also, burning just after the start of the rains to reduce ticks – elderly Africans claimed a big increase in ticks after Europeans prevented burning.*)

Whelan, R.J. **(2002)** Don't fight fire with fire. Letter to Nature 416(15). (*Would this letter be an interesting subject for question-mapping?*)

Whewell, W. **(1840)** The History of the Inductive Sciences. Cass, London 1967. (*Whewell was a polymath who coined the words 'consilience' and 'scientist'.*)

Whitehurst, R. **(1992)** *Noongar* Dictionary, *Noongar* Language and Culture Centre, Perth, Western Australia. (*A most useful source.*)

Williams, C.D.H. **(1998)** How to boil an egg. New Scientist Magazine, April 4th. (*A mathematical model in all its glory.*)

Wilson, E.O. **(1998)** Consilience: The Unity of Knowledge. Alfred A. Knopf, New York. (*Book that discusses 'consilience', but Whewell might not have entirely agreed with it.*)

Wilson, T. **(1560)** The Arte of Rhetorique. Ed. G.H. Mair, Oxford, Clarendon Press, (1909). (*Noted logician and rhetorician at Cambridge University in the time of Queen Elizabeth the First of England.*)

Wu, J. and Loucks, O.L. **(1995)** From balance of nature to hierarchical patch dynamics: a paradigm shift in ecology. The Quarterly Review of Biology **70**(4): 439-466. (*Supports fire patch mosaics.*)

Yankelovich, D. **(1972)** Corporate Priorites. Stanford CT: Yankelovich Inc. (*Clearly pointed out the futility of trying to reduce social and historical complexity to a simplistic mathematical model.*)

-oOo-

Index of Humans Involved

Few, if any authors, can claim to be the sole source of ideas used in their books. It is amazing how many people contribute to a book, even if they are unaware of, and sometimes not thanked for, their contribution. I am aware of over a hundred contributors given below, but I might have missed a few. Only some of these are in the bibliography above. I thank those who are alive, and salute those who are now dead.

Readers should have few difficulties with abbreviations. I am only aware of three which may puzzle readers who are not from Australia, namely AFSM (Australian Fire Service Medal), SRC (Swan River Colony), and WA (Western Australia).

Abbott, Dr. Ian, D.Sc., a reliable WA scientist.
Aristotle, cross disciplinary Greek philosopher.
Backhouse, James, Quaker traveller who visited Perth, WA, in 1837.
Bacon, Alice, Lady, wife of Francis Bacon
Bacon, Francis, Lord Verulam, English philosopher and essayist.
Barlee, Hon. F., early secretary of SRC .
Bates, Daisy, Irish journalist, friend to Aboriginal people.
Bierce, Ambrose, American cynic with some interesting views on philosophy.
Bland, Richard. Protector of Natives SRC.
Broome, Governor of SRC.
Broun, Peter, Secretary of SRC.
Brynyard, South African with knowledge of Kruger National Park.
Budiansky, Stephen, distinguished and helpful American historian.
Bunbury, Lt. Henry, military officer SRC.
Burchell, W.F., early African explorer
Burns, Robert, forthright and much loved Scottish poet.
Burrows, Dr. Neil, AFSM, bushfire scientist, WA.
Chatwin, Bruce, English writer interested in songlines.
Checkland, Prof. Peter, devised Soft Systems Research.

129

Cicero, Marcus Tullius. Roman philosopher, lawyer, and essayist.

Clarke, Col. Andrew, Governor of SRC.

Clements, ecologist, in 1936 proposed the unconvincing 'Vegetation Climax Theory' of ecology.

Cook, Thomas, travel agent.

Cornwall, Koodah, *Noongar* Elder with a sense of humour.

Darwin, Charles, author of 'Origin of Species'.

de Montaine, Michel, French essayist.

Dinely, Colonial Surgeon, SRC.

Dionysius of Halicarnassus, Greek philosopher of history, c. 30 BC.

Drummond, James, botanist, SRC.

Eliot, George, early resident at Bunbury, SRC.

Ferguson, Euan, AFSM, Australian bushfire manager.

Fisher, Sir Ronald, English statistician.

Galton, Francis, English statistician.

Gardner, Charles A., long serving WA state botanist.

Gould, Stephen J., American humanist scholar.

Govender, Navashni, former manager at Kruger National Park.

Gowers, Sir Ernest, expert on plain English.

Gratte, Stan, long term bushman around Eneabba, WA.

Grove, T.S., reliable Australian scientist.

Hallam, Professor Sylvia, reliable Australian anthropologist.

Hammond, J.F., writer on *Noongar* history.

Harris, Alan. C., Conservator of Forests, WA..

Hegel, Georg W.F., German philosopher.

Hume, David, Scottish philosopher.

Hutchins, Sir David, eccentric forest consultant who visited WA..

Irwin, Frederick C., Governor SRC.

Jones, Julie, Department of Aboriginal and Torres State Islander Affairs, WA.

Kelly, Glenn, member of well-known *Noongar* family, interested in fire.

Kelly, Lynne, writer on Aboriginal songlines.

Kessel, Stephen, Conservator of Forests, WA.

Kipling, Rudyard, English author.

Kozlowski, T.T., American expert on fire effect upon soil and bacteria.

Kull, Christian, studied traditional use of fire in Madagascar, including attempt by French colonial government to ban it.

Lane-Poole, Charles, Conservator of Forests, WA.

Mackey, Prof., Brendan, has dismissed fire as a way of reducing heavy fuel.

Marchetti, Elaine, descendant of old grazier family in *tuart* forest, WA..

Marshall, noted widespread fire in Africa, lit by humans.

Marwick, studied *Swazi* fire vocabulary in Africa.

McCaw, Dr. Lachlan, bushfire research scientist, WA.

McNamara, Robert, American politician and statistician.

Meares, Captain Richard, early settler in SRC at York.

Midgely, Professor Mary, English philosopher.

Milligan, Spike, Anglo-Irish comedian and wit.

Molloy, Georgiana, early settler in SRC.

Molloy, Lt. Col. John, magistrate in SRC, husband of Georgiana.

Monger, Hon., politician of SRC who recognised *Noongar* need for kangaroo meat.

Nannup, Dr. Noel OAM, *Noongar* Elder.

Neale, Margot, Aboriginal writer on songlines.

Orwell, George, clear English thinker and writer.

Parkington, J., noted historical description of burning by *Soaqua* people of South Africa.

Pell, Prof., interested in statistics of parachute trials. I

Plato, Greek philosopher, noted the importance of knowledge gained by practical experience.

Plutarch, Greek philosopher, essayist, historian, and biographer.

Popper, Professor Karl, Anglo-Austrian philosopher.

Preiss, Ludwig, German botanist.

Pyne, Professor Stephen, American, the world's best fire historian and philosopher.

Quêtelet, Adolphe, Belgian statistician.

Quinton, Lord Robert, expert on Francis Bacon.

Ribet, Dr. Helene, greatly interested in traditional use of fire in France.

Rogers, Dr. Carl, American humanist and psychologist.

Rogers, Dr., early Colonial Medical Officer, SRC.

Salvado, Dom Rosendo, early Spanish missionary in SRC.

Schapera, early South African explorer, noted burning by Africans for hunting and grass stimulation.

Shenton, Hon., politician of SRC who knew of *Noongar* need for kangaroo meat.

Singleton, Francis Corbet, SRC landowner and observer of *Noongar* use of fire.

Smith, Prof., interested in statistics of parachute trials.

Snow, Dr. Charles, Percy, English author of 'Two Cultures', a book on science and humanities.

Stamp, Donald B.A., schoolteacher who loved clear English.

Stephenson-Hamilton, J. Colonel, onetime superintendent of Kruger National Park.

Stokes, Captain Henry, Royal Navy, first hand observer of *Noongar* burning near Albany.

Symmons, Charles, Protector of Natives, SRC.

Thompson, Frank, settled on south coast of Western Australia before World War 1.

Verulam, Lord (See Francis Bacon).

Vickers, Sir Geoffrey, English soldier, creative scientist, and philosopher, who warned against ignoring the importance of human qualities.

Vico, Professor Giovanni Batista, Italian philosopher.

Voltaire, French essayist, historian and philosopher

Waylen, Colonial Surgeon, SRC.

Wellington, Duke of, British soldier, won the Battle of Waterloo.

West, Oliver, former Rhodesian ecologist.

Whelan, Prof., Robert, has claimed that fire should not be fought with fire.

Whewell, Professor William, philosopher and scientist.

Whitehurst, Rosemary, author of *Noongar* Dictionary.

Williams, Dr. Charles H., created a mathematical model of egg boiling.

Williams, Robin, American actor.

Wilson, Thomas, English Elizabethan scholar who loved rhetoric and logic.

Wilson, Dr. J.B., Colonial Surgeon, SRC.

Winjan, nineteenth century *Noongar* Elder.

Wollaston, Rev. John, Anglican priest, noted frequency and extent of bushfires in his day.

Wood, William, early settler in America (1639).

Yeats, William Butler, Irish poet.

-oOo-

About the Author

Due to my father's military career, I attended eight different schools, including one in Addis Ababa, and two in Egypt. All this rather confused me, although I did learn a few words of Amharic and Arabic. It took me until I was thirty years old to sort things out.

Once I discovered essayists such as Francis Bacon, I began to enjoy essay writing, and realised that it could help to sort out some false logic noticed by Aristotle. I will continue to draw attention to what I think are dangerous errors in some refereed scientific papers on bushfire. I do believe that they could get people, and both domestic and wild animals killed.